MADE IN ITALY
DAVID ROCCO

By *the same author:*
David Rocco's Dolce Vita

MADE IN ITALY
DAVID ROCCO

Photography by Francesco Lastrucci

Additional photography by Rutendo Sabeta

Clarkson Potter/Publishers
New York

Published in the United States by Clarkson Potter/
Publishers, an imprint of the Crown Publishing Group,
a division of Random House, Inc., New York.
www.crownpublishing.com
www.clarksonpotter.com

CLARKSON POTTER is a trademark and POTTER with
colophon is a registered trademark of Random House, Inc.

Simultaneously published in Canada by
HarperCollins Publishers Ltd., Toronto.

All photographs by Francesco Lastrucci, except the
following: Rutendo Sabeta, pages 74–87, 101,130–131,
134–135, 142–143,146–147, 154–156, 158–159, 160–161,
170–173, 177–185, 222, 226, 244, 284–287, 292–297,
301–302, 304–311, 336–337, 357, 366–368, 370–375, 377;
and Geoff George, pages 330, 331; and the photographs
on pages 39 and 319.

Library of Congress Cataloging-in-Publication Data
is available upon request.

ISBN 978-0-307-88922-5

Printed in China

10 9 8 7 6 5 4 3 2 1

First U.S. Edition

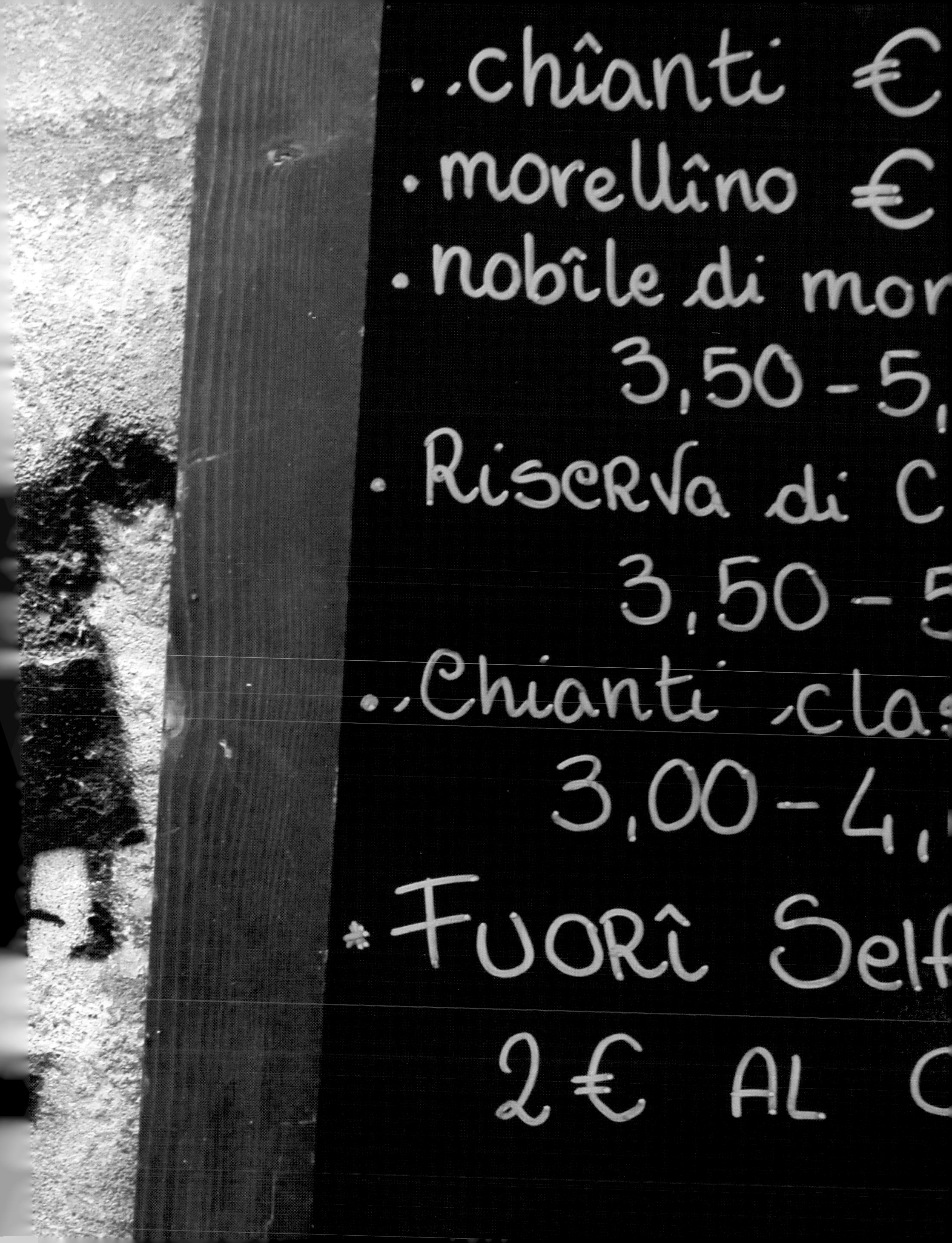

- ..chîanti €
- morellîno €
- nobîle di mor
  3,50 - 5,
- Riserva di C
  3,50 - 5
- ..Chianti cla
  3,00 - 4,
- Fuorî Self
  2€ AL

To my delicious
Emma-bunny & Giorgia-girl.
My inspirations.

Contents

Introduction

I always say that being Italian, cooking is in my DNA. I grew up in a house where going into the kitchen and helping out was completely natural and easy. Nothing was very fancy. We made traditional Italian food that my parents learned from their parents. We'd hang out together, cook together, eat together—so the kitchen was also a place of real connection.

Some people think cooking has to be complicated to be good. But in my experience, the exact opposite is true.

When you write a cookbook, you put your philosophy and beliefs out there and hope that they resonate with people. I'm always a little nervous about communicating my approach, because I'm very visual and intuitive in the kitchen. At times I worry whether people will understand what a "handful of this" or a "splash of that" will mean and whether they'll be able to make it work for them. But that's part of the tradition and heritage of the kitchen that is important to me. Strict measurements don't work for me, and for sure cooking would be a lot less fun if I had to use them. And besides, I'm not classically trained—I'm Italian trained!

And so I've been incredibly touched and encouraged by the responses I've had to my first book.

Of course, you hope that what you write will inspire people to get into the kitchen. But what I didn't expect were the letters from people who said, "You know, I'm so sorry that I didn't write down my grandmother's or my mother's recipes. I've missed their food. And your style of cooking is very similar. So I feel like I've reconnected with their food and got a piece of them back in the process."

I make no secret about the fact that I am inspired by old-school, traditional, peasant-style Italian cooking. I say it over and over again: it's simple, delicious and timeless.

So when I set out to write this book, I decided to go on a road trip through parts of Italy where I have friends and extended family. I wanted to reconnect with the people, places and food that excite me and bring to life some of the recipes I enjoyed along the way.

Here's the irony about Italy: Italians—who are known for their leading-edge style, their fashion and design, and who love making *la bella figura* and being peacocks—are, when it comes to food, traditionalists. Simplicity in the kitchen is understood. They're not looking for a new spin on their pasta. They know what a good tomato sauce should taste like, and it's respected and appreciated. Italy is a country of contradictions—breathtakingly beautiful and yet seriously dysfunctional and disorganized. But when it comes to philosophy about food, regional preferences notwithstanding, Italians can all sit together at the same table.

And when you go looking for food in Italy, you inevitably meet great characters, too.

One day, after a morning at the beach, I had lunch at a friend's restaurant in Ravello, on the Amalfi coast. We were joined by a friend of his, an intimidating-looking guy with a gruff voice. But when he found out that I was writing a book, his gruffness disappeared. He immediately pulled out his *telefonino* and completely rearranged his afternoon because he wanted to show me *his* Costiera Amalfitana.

He called himself the *Buon Gustaio*—a man of taste. So, to show that I respected his time, I said, "Okay, *va bene! Sono pronto. Andiamo!*" "No, no!" he said, raising his hands. "We have to be 'civilized' and do things right. First we have espresso. Then our digestivo. And *then* we go!"

The next five hours was a marathon of generosity and food. We drove all over the region, making stops along the way at little shops where I met the people who make the best bread, the best homemade wine, salami, pizza, cookies, etc., etc. Everywhere, the Buon Gustaio was greeted like an old friend—and because I was with him, so was I! He introduced me to the family who, he said, made the best fior di latte in the region. The third generation, the kids now running the business, wear Gucci and Prada, even to milk the sheep. They struck me as so quintessentially Italian, with their mix of cutting-edge fashion and their unwavering respect for the old-world style of making this luscious cheese.

And if this weren't enough, the Buon Gustaio picked up his cellphone, called his wife and said, "*Butta la pasta. Abbiamo un amico che cena con noi.*" The phrase *butta la pasta* put a smile on my face. I had thought it was a Rocco thing, because it was the exact phrase my dad would use when he'd call my mom as he was leaving work, so the pasta would be ready by the time he got home.

Entering the Buon Gustaio's house was like walking into my mom's or my aunts'. His wife greeted me with open arms. We sat at the table for hours, eating fantastic food inspired by Amalfitana and Neapolitan traditional cooking and then engaging in hours more of conversations about food.

Not only are Italians proud to feed you, but they're proud to share recipes and techniques. It doesn't matter if they're chefs, lawyers or government workers. Most of them love food, know their way around the kitchen and have an opinion on how things are done. They're schooled by the experience that comes from generations of families cooking and eating together.

Italians are famously regional in their attitudes, and you'll really see this in the way they make even signature dishes of a particular area. Sometimes they're *provinciale* to a fault and will be absolutely closed-minded about a dish that's made differently in a town just eighty miles away. One of the blessings of my job is that I travel all over Italy and experience the foods of many different regions, so I have an openness that many Italians don't.

Let me tell you a story about Italians and regional bias: *Caponata* is one of the quintessential signature dishes of Sicily, so you'd think there would be a definitive version. When a successful Northern Italian chef was about to open a new restaurant in the Sicilian port town of Sciacca and wanted to offer caponata on the menu, he

wanted to make sure it was *autentico*. He asked a friend of mine who works in the food industry if he could come over and learn how to make the family's caponata.

With typical Sicilian hospitality, my friend said, "Of course!" and invited his sisters and his aunt over to the house as well to meet the chef. First there were introductions and a discussion; then, very quickly, someone gave a recipe. This was followed by someone else correcting them, and then another opinion, and within a very short time, the room had become so loud and so full of opinions that even the chef was worked up.

Why the fuss over a dish of eggplant and capers? Well, this story gives us an insight into the Italian attitude towards food: Make food you love, and make it your own. And then defend it—even to a professional chef!

In my mind, a cookbook is not a bible. It should be an inspiration.

My recipes are simple, and I take pride in the fact that anyone can make them, whether you're a five-star chef or a first-timer. They don't discriminate. These recipes are *Made in Italy*.

Quanto Basta

Quanto Basta (QB) is a cooking philosophy that suggests that you use "as much as you need" or "as much as you want" to make a recipe work for your taste. I love this freedom. In my younger years, when I was first traveling through Italy and absorbing the cooking, I would ask how much of something I needed to make a recipe. Inevitably there would be a shrug of the shoulders and a wave of the hands, and the answer would be *"Ma … quanto basta."* In fact, you'll often find QB—or no measurements at all—in Italian cookbooks, because it's taken for granted that you'll make the dish your own.

For example, when it comes to an ingredient like flour for a pizza dough, if your hands and eyes are telling you that you still need more, that the dough isn't uniform yet, then keep adding a little at a time until you get to the right texture. Use your senses.

Use as much as you want or need. This is *quanto basta*, and it's my philosophy of cooking.

What You Need to Know

For me, cooking is a passion and a pleasure. And if anything, my hope is that I can either add to your pleasure in the kitchen or convince the reluctant among you to find your way in to something I think will enrich your life. Watching people enjoy even a simple dish you've prepared is energizing. It's one of the best ways to bring a little joy into the world. Trust me on this.

I like to say that there are no rules in the kitchen, but obviously there are some basics. However, nothing in this book requires anything fancy. If you can turn on a stove and use a spoon to stir, you can use these recipes. I don't use many gadgets. I prefer to chop things by hand or with a mezzaluna. I have a blender, but for the most part I like the sensuality of connecting with my food and watching the dishes develop in front of me. It's a relaxing and creative experience for me, and that's what cooking should be.

And I encourage you to make these recipes your own. I'm all about putting your own spin on a recipe. It's about *your* taste buds, not mine. Feel free to substitute ingredients that you prefer. And don't let the lack of an ingredient stop you from making something. In this book, I've included a number of soups that you can make with just water. If you have stock on hand, you can use it, but the soups are also beautiful and tasty if you follow the recipes just as written.

Things like the climate and humidity of where you live, and the ingredients and brands you use, will also affect the outcome of your recipe. I know that when I make dough in Italy, it's different from making the same recipe in Toronto, where the climate is different. The efficiency of your pots and pans, and oven temperature, also come into play. My oven's 350°F may be different from your oven's 350°F. If your eyes are telling you the food is done before the time indicated in the recipe, trust your eyes.

The issue of al dente pasta freaks some people out, but finding the al dente point in your pasta will change your life! There's a difference between raw and al dente. Your pasta should have a soft outside but not flop like a rice noodle when you bite into it. You want it to stand up to a sauce, not disintegrate into it. I'd suggest checking your pasta a few minutes before the time given on the package. And I almost always finish cooking my pasta with the sauce. The pasta releases starches into the sauce so that it combines and clings to the pasta—which really brings the dish together.

People are also surprised to see me liberally salt the water in which I'm about to cook pasta. But this is where the pasta gets its seasoning. And you do it liberally because the pasta will absorb only a fraction of what you put in. So don't be afraid to add a tablespoon or two.

Salting a dish is something people are very sensitive about, partly because of taste issues, and partly because of health concerns. There are a few things to know: First of all, salt as you go, a little at a time, especially if you're a beginner. You can always add more to a dish in its final stages, but you can't take salt away. If you are using ingredients that are really salty, like anchovies or Parmigiano-Reggiano cheese, then keep that in mind when you're salting your dish. Anchovies are often used at the beginning of a cooked dish partly for their saltiness, and Parmigiano is often used at the end to finish the dish. So again, use your judgment. And by the way, in my kitchen, salt is either sea salt or kosher salt.

Because I love to go freestyle as much as possible in the kitchen, baking is not a big part of my repertoire, as it does require that you pay attention to measurements. When it comes to desserts, and especially baking, my recipes are forgiving as well, but they are more specific.

I'll talk more about this later, but when I say olive oil, I always mean extra-virgin olive oil. It's the only oil I use in my kitchen. It's the same with cheese; Parmigiano-Reggiano can't be replaced by something that shakes out of a can. I know price sometimes sends people to the cheaper option, but the flavor and joy you get out of good food is like nothing else and to me is worth it. Pay for the real thing and you get true taste, no fillers—and often, a little goes a long way.

My inspiration is the tradition of *cucina povera*, or peasant cuisine, where not a scrap was allowed to go to waste. So, dried pieces of cheese go into a potato dish or help flavor a soup. Old bread is an opportunity to add a new flavor or texture to a dish. To me, that speaks about respecting the food, the people who produce it, and in the end, yourself.

Aperitivi

Un *aperitivo* can be anything from a cocktail to a glass of wine, generally enjoyed before the meal.

In spite of the amount of wine that Italians consume, I don't think of them as big drinkers. I think of them as sophisticated drinkers.

They'll stop at a bar on their way home from work for an aperitivo and decompress from the day, which is probably more about meeting and socializing than about drinking. The Italian attitude to alcohol is about sensuality and community.

In Italy, the bar is where locals go to see and be seen over drinks, and young fashionistas stop to show off their tans and get in some post-work flirting before heading to a restaurant to meet friends or going home to the family dinner.

The bar is a great place to appreciate the casually elegant style for which Italy is famous. I think of it as "the uniform"— Gucci meets Diesel, and the footwear of choice is Tod's or Hogan.

For Italian fashionistas, God has always been in the details. I consider this a metaphor for the style of drinks.

PANZANELLA COCKTAIL

My pal Matteo, who owns and tends bar at the trendy Dolce Vita in Piazza del Carmine in Florence, came up with this clever take on the classic Tuscan Panzanella salad.

1/2 lime, quartered	6 fresh basil leaves
1 tbsp (15 mL) sugar	2 oz (60 mL) vodka
4 cucumber slices, 1/2 inch (1 cm) thick, peeled	Ice
	Ginger ale

In a glass, mash or muddle the lime, sugar, 1 cucumber slice and basil. Add vodka and ice, mix well, and top with ginger ale and remaining cucumber slices.

Per 1 persona

KIWI GRAPEFRUIT COCKTAIL

Although the fruit's name probably makes you think of New Zealand, Italy is actually one of the world's leading producers of kiwi.

1/2 fresh kiwi, peeled	Ice
Touch of kiwi syrup or simple syrup	Fresh grapefruit juice
2 oz (60 mL) vodka	

In a cocktail shaker, muddle kiwi and add syrup, vodka and ice. Shake well, pour into a glass (with or without ice, your choice) and top with grapefruit juice.

Per 1 persona

MILANO-TORINO, AKA AMERICANO

This drink was first served in the 1860s at a bar in Milan called Caffè Campari. (The gent who created it, Gaspare Campari, is the guy who invented Campari.) If you'd ordered it in the late 1800s, you would have asked for it by its original name, Milano-Torino. It was called that because the Campari came from Milan, the Vermouth from Torino. But because of its popularity with American tourists, it became known by its nickname, Americano.

1 1/2 oz (45 mL) sweet vermouth	Chilled club soda, to taste
1 1/2 oz (45 mL) Campari	Orange peel, for garnish

In a glass, mix the vermouth and Campari. Top up with club soda and add a twist of orange peel.

Per 1 persona

NEGRONI/NEGRONI SBAGLIATO

I like this a lot. But when I drink it outside of Italy, I get razzed by my friends, who think that its pretty color means that I'm drinking something one step up from a Shirley Temple. Well, I'm here to tell you that they don't know jack.

The Negroni is a sophisticated, tasty aperitivo that delivers a kick. It will give you a nice buzz and excite your appetite. So man up, boys. Paper umbrella optional.

In Milan they drink the Negroni Sbagliato, which means "Negroni with a mistake." They use prosecco instead of gin. The drink isn't as strong as the classic Negroni, but it's just as tasty.

1 part gin	1 part Italian sweet vermouth
1 part Campari	ice (optional)

The formula is equal parts of all three ingredients, which can be served straight up or over ice.

Per 1 persona

The following drinks are classic Italian: simple and delicious. They are all a mix of prosecco and fruit juice. You could also substitute Spumanti *dolce* (sweet) or *secco* (dry) for the prosecco. All of the ingredients should be cold.

ARANCE SANGUIGNE E PROSECCO
BLOODY MIMOSA

1 part freshly squeezed blood-orange juice (or regular orange juice)

2 parts prosecco

POMPELMO ROSA E PROSECCO
PINK GRAPEFRUIT AND PROSECCO

1 part freshly squeezed pink grapefruit juice

2 parts prosecco

MELAGRANA E PROSECCO
POMEGRANATE AND PROSECCO

You can use bottled or fresh pomegranate juice. Squeeze pomegranates as you would oranges. Just make sure they're very ripe.

1 part pomegranate juice

2 parts prosecco

ITALIAN SPRITZ

For a long time, the Spritz was served exclusively in Northern Italy, but in the last few years it's migrated throughout the rest of Italy and Europe. The fact that the Italian liqueur Aperol is low in alcohol makes this an easy, breezy cocktail you can have at any time of the day, and it's perfect for a hot summer afternoon. I was introduced to the drink in Sicily and must have had it every day for three weeks straight. I highly recommend serving it, as the Sicilians do, with fresh mint leaves.

Ice	Club soda
2 oz (60 mL) Aperol	1 slice orange, for garnish
3 oz (90 mL) prosecco	Fresh mint leaves

Put some ice in a glass, add your alcohol, top up with club soda and give it a stir. Garnish with the orange slice and mint leaves.

Per 1 persona

DOLCE VITA SURUBAO

This is one of the signature drinks at Bar Dolce Vita in Florence. *Surubao* in Portuguese means "orgy," and bar owner Matteo says this drink is an orgy of flavor.

7 fresh raspberries

3 fresh blackberries

1 tbsp (15 mL) raspberry syrup

1 tbsp (15 mL) sugar

Juice of 1/2 lime, freshly
   squeezed

2 oz (60 mL) vodka

4 oz (125 mL)
   cranberry juice

Crushed ice

1 slice lime, for garnish

Put your raspberries, blackberries, raspberry syrup, sugar and lime juice into a large glass. With your muddler, mash and mix all the ingredients together. Then add vodka, cranberry juice and crushed ice to taste. Garnish with a slice of lime.

Per 1 persona

ITALIAN MOJITO

This is a twist on the classic Mojito, substituting prosecco for soda water. Don't let the pretty pink straws in the photo fool you—this is a big boy's drink.

1/2 lime, quartered	1 oz (30 mL) white rum
2 tsp (10 mL) sugar	Ice cubes
6–7 large fresh mint leaves	Prosecco

In a glass, bash together lime, sugar and mint leaves. Add rum and ice cubes and top with prosecco.

Per 1 persona

Antipasti
Insalate
Contorni

A*ntipasti* are starters, *insalate* are salads, and *contorni* are sides. And any and all of them can be eaten as snacks.

This chapter is a mishmash, and it reflects my style of eating. For me, it's not about rules or rigid definitions of what should come before *un risotto* or alongside *una bistecca*. I don't think it's a big deal if you serve *un contorno* as a part of *gli antipasti* or make a meal out of it with some good bread and a glass of vino.

AVOCADO CAPRESE

This is a twist on the classic Caprese salad. The first time I had it, I was sitting on the terrace of the Hotel Villa Maria in Ravello, which overlooks the gorgeous Amalfi coast.

A traditional Caprese marries sweet, vine-ripened tomatoes in season with fresh, creamy fior di latte and brings the flavors together with excellent olive oil and fresh basil. This version adds the lush richness of avocado. It's one of those perfect summer dishes, a salad that gives you the feeling of satisfaction of having a meal that sometimes other salads don't. This is not a recipe per se—these are just the components. Put them together in the way that suits your taste. It's all *quanto basta*, as much as you need and want. Just be sure to use your best olive oil.

1 avocado, sliced
2 fresh tomatoes, sliced
2 large balls fior di latte, sliced
4 fresh basil leaves

Salt, QB
Dried oregano, QB (optional)
Extra-virgin olive oil, QB

Per 2 persone

INSALATA DI POMODORI E MELONE
TOMATO MELON SALAD

I love using sweet fruit in a savory salad. You'll find this a lot in Sicily. There, people "get" mixing these flavors. That may be a result of how incredible their fruit is. I'm going to give you the basics to match the picture, but don't be afraid to make this salad your own. For instance, you don't have to use arugula as a base. Sometimes I use only fruit, some finely chopped red onion for spice and heat, and some fresh mint or oregano.

You can change up the fruit. I've used melon here, but oranges or figs are also great. The thing that brings all the flavors together is the olive oil, so use the good stuff here.

2 or 3 medium vine-ripened tomatoes	4 tbsp (60 mL) extra-virgin olive oil
1 cucumber, peeled and sliced	Salt and freshly ground pepper, QB
1/2 cantaloupe, peeled and diced	Dried oregano, QB (optional)
1/4 red onion, diced	1 bunch arugula, torn
1–2 tbsp (15–30 mL) red wine vinegar	

The key here is to mix your tomatoes, cucumber, melon and red onions in the vinegar, oil and spices and let that sit for 5 minutes. Make sure, though, that you don't overdo it with the oregano or the red wine vinegar. These are really just slight complements to the fruit and the fantastic olive oil, and too much of either will overpower the dish.

On a serving platter, lay out your greens. I prefer using baby arugula because it has a nice pepperiness and makes a great base for the salad. Add the seasoned fruits and vegetables on top. Serve immediately.

Per 4 persone

COUSCOUS ALLA PANZANELLA
COUSCOUS PANZANELLA

This is a clever variation on the Tuscan bread salad, *panzanella*. It's easy to make, and the best thing is that, like the bread salad from which it draws its name, there's no cooking. You make it right in the serving bowl.

People are always surprised to hear that couscous is part of Italian cooking. But it is, especially in Sicily, where in certain areas it's used more than conventional pasta, and they even have couscous festivals.

With this dish, you can go super rustic and serve it on a big platter. Or do what I do for a more elegant affair: fill a teacup with the couscous, packing it down slightly; then, on a beautiful white dish, invert the teacup, tap the bottom and unmold.

1/2 cup (125 mL) extra-virgin olive oil

Juice of 1 lemon

2 cups (500 mL) canned, peeled plum tomatoes, chopped, with juices

1 red onion, chopped

1 red pepper, chopped

1 yellow pepper, chopped

10 cherry tomatoes, quartered

1 bunch fresh basil leaves, torn

Salt and freshly ground pepper, QB

2 cups (500 mL) couscous

You can make couscous in boiling water in 5 minutes. But in this case, you're going to let your raw couscous rehydrate by absorbing the flavorful liquids of the salad. So, in a big serving bowl, make a liquid base of olive oil, lemon juice, plum tomatoes and juices, red onions, red and yellow peppers, cherry tomatoes, half of the basil, and salt and pepper. Pour the uncooked couscous right into the middle of the bowl and mix it with the other ingredients very, very well. I suggest using your hands for this so you're really sure that the couscous is mixed thoroughly. Let the couscous sit in the fridge until it has absorbed all the liquid, which will take a couple of hours. About halfway through, give it another good mix. The longer it sits, the better it will be. In fact, if I'm going to serve this at night, I make it in the morning. When the couscous is ready, add the rest of the basil and mix thoroughly.

Per 4 persone

INSALATA DI FINOCCHIO
FENNEL SALAD

I love fennel. It was always part of our holiday meals, when we would eat way more of everything than seemed humanly possible. My mom said about fennel, *aiuto a digerire*—it helps you digest and allows you to continue the marathon of food. Or it can be served on its own after dinner. I'm not sure it helps digestion, but I do know it offers a refreshing crunch at break and mealtime.

1 large fennel bulb

1 small red onion

1 cup (250 mL) fresh blueberries

1/4 cup (60 mL) extra-virgin olive oil

Juice of 1 orange

Salt and freshly ground pepper, QB

Wash your fennel, cut off stems and fronds. Discard the stems, and set the fronds aside for a garnish, if you want. With a mandolin or a knife, cut the fennel bulb into very thin slices. Dice the red onion. Put the fennel and onion into a mixing bowl and add the blueberries. Now add olive oil, orange juice, salt and pepper, and mix it all together. This dish can be made in advance or served immediately. The fennel won't lose its firmness and will absorb the flavors. I often substitute pomegranate seeds, when in season, for the blueberries. They give the dish a beautiful color and add a nice crunch and tartness.

Per 4 persone

INSALATA DI ORZO
BARLEY SALAD

I've made this salad with both barley and farro; the two are quite similar. Both are beautiful grains that have a chewy, firm texture. This makes them perfect for salads, because they hold their integrity for a long time, even after the salad has been dressed. They're very digestible and light, and even some people with wheat or gluten intolerances can handle them. This salad is simple—with big-time results. And it will keep in the fridge for a few days.

1 1/4 cups (310 mL) barley or farro	4 tbsp (60 mL) extra-virgin olive oil
1 red pepper	Chili pepper flakes, QB
1 yellow pepper	
1 large carrot	Red Wine Vinegar Reduction:
1 zucchini	2 cups (500 mL) red wine vinegar
2 spring onions, chopped	1 tbsp (15 mL) sugar
1 clove garlic, finely chopped	

The cooking method for both grains is exactly the same. The ratio is two to one: 2 cups (500 mL) water to 1 cup (250 mL) grain. You don't need to prerinse either. Put your barley or farro into a pot with cold water, bring to a boil, reduce the heat to medium-high and let it cook for about 20 minutes. The texture will be somewhat chewy, but firm.

For the rest of the salad, thinly cut or julienne the vegetables. Then heat up 2 tbsp (30 mL) of the olive oil and quickly stir-fry the vegetables with the chili flakes. Make sure you don't overcook them—you want them slightly crisp. When they're done, add them to the farro or barley. Season with the remaining olive oil, salt and pepper, and a couple of tablespoons (30 mL) of the red wine vinegar reduction. The reduction is intense, and a little goes a long way. You can serve this dish warm or chilled.

To make your red vinegar reduction: Put the red wine vinegar in a pot with the sugar. Stir to help dissolve the sugar and, over high heat, bring your mixture to a boil. Then turn the heat down to medium and let it simmer until the vinegar reduces to a third. This will make more than you need for this recipe, but it keeps well in the fridge.

Per 4 persone

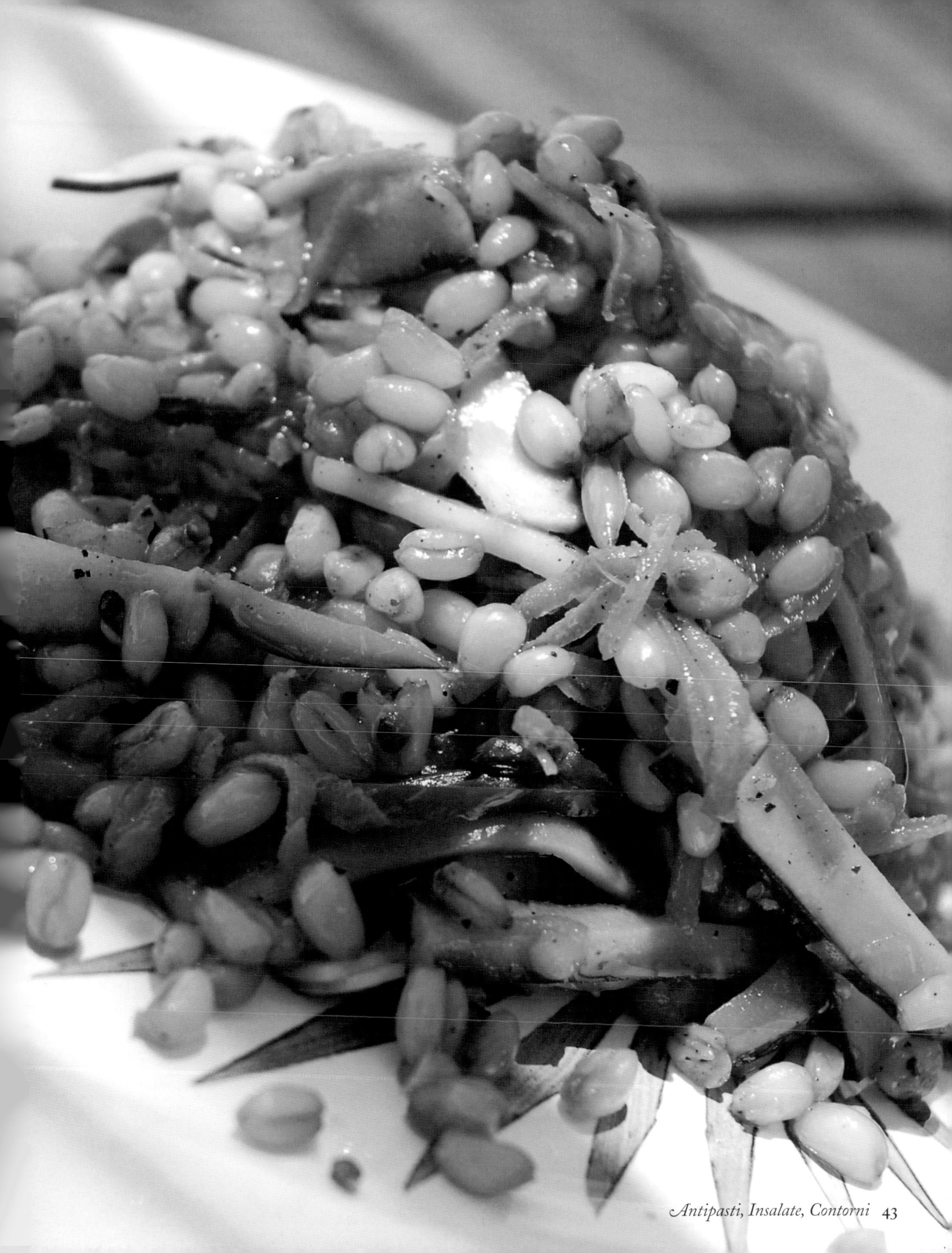

MERCATO

Palermo Markets

Palermo is a sophisticated city, a historic city, a culturally rich city with lots to do and see. But whenever I'm there, I find myself drawn back to the markets. There are three: Vucciria, Ballarò and Capo. They're anything but glamorous and don't strive to be anything other than what they've been for centuries. In fact, they look like they've been jammed into back alleys against a backdrop of old and crumbling buildings.

The Palermo markets are an assault on the senses—the vibrant colors of the fruits and vegetables, the smell of the fish stalls, the grinding noise of the Vespas that cut their way through the crowds.

The vendors are great characters. You hear them yell back and forth to each other; this is street theater. Talk to them once, and they remember you forever. The people who bring the food to the market are generally the ones who grow it or produce it. Chefs may be celebrities—but these folks are the real stars.

The old markets in Italy are all an experience, and if you want to find the soul of the city, head over to one of them.

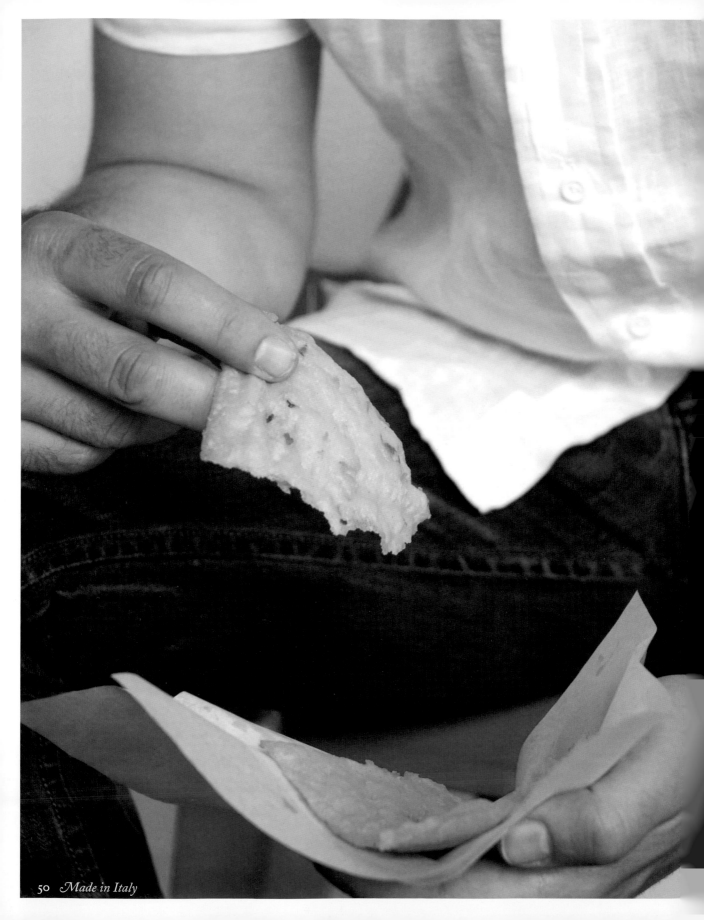

PANELLA DEL MERCATO BALLARÒ
BALLARÒ MARKET CHICKPEA FRITTERS

This is true street food that's been served the same way for centuries in Sicilian open-air markets. You buy this from street vendors, who hand it to you to eat on its own as a fritter, or in a bun with some grated pecorino and a squeeze of lemon. You can also find this treat in Tuscany, where it's called *la cecina*. The difference is that panella is deep-fried, and la cecina is baked in an oven, like a pizza. If you go the Tuscan route and bake it in an oven, make sure to preheat the pan and the olive oil so that when the chickpea flour goes in, it will "fry" a little bit as it bakes to a nice golden brown.

2 cups (500 mL) chickpea flour	1 tbsp (15 mL) salt
4 cups (1 L) cold water	A pinch of freshly ground pepper
1/2 cup (125 mL) extra-virgin olive oil	Parsley, QB

This is really simple. Mix the chickpea flour with cold water, a couple of tablespoons (30 mL) of olive oil, and a little bit of salt, pepper and parsley until you get an even, pancake-like batter. Let the mixture rest for about 1 hour.

If you're cooking it in the oven, preheat the oven to 450°F (230°C).

Spread the remaining olive oil on a 16-inch (40 cm) pizza pan, and let it heat up before you pour in the batter. Once the pan is hot, pour the batter into the center; it will spread out on its own. Cook for 25 minutes, or until golden brown.

If you're frying the mixture, pour the olive oil into a deep frying pan. When the oil is hot, drop the batter in and fry until golden. Remove to a paper towel to absorb the excess oil.

Per 6–8 persone

PATATE E FAGIOLINI
POTATOES AND GREEN BEANS

There's nothing glamorous about this recipe, but it's so delicious that friends of mine served it at their wedding. It's a thing of simple beauty.

4 potatoes, peeled and cut into eighths

1 lb (500 g) green beans, trimmed

3/4 cup (175 mL) extra-virgin olive oil

Zest and juice of 1–2 lemons

Salt and freshly ground pepper, QB

4 fresh basil leaves, torn

Boil potatoes until tender, about 10 to 15 minutes. Drain.

Bring a separate pot of water to a boil, drop in the beans and cook until tender, about 5 minutes. Drain, gently pat dry and add them to the potatoes.

Pour olive oil into a bowl, squeeze in lemon juice, add some salt and pepper, the basil leaves and lemon zest, and give it all a mix. Pour this over the vegetables and toss gently to coat. Let sit 30 minutes before serving.

Per 4–6 persone

INSALATA DI FAGIOLINI
GREEN BEAN SALAD

Green beans are such a versatile vegetable. They hold their integrity when cooked and will absorb and enhance the flavors of whatever you mix with them. I recommend making this salad in advance. I prefer to eat it the day after making it, as the beans absorb all the flavors.

2 lb (1 kg) green beans, trimmed

5 tbsp (75 mL) extra-virgin olive oil

8 fresh mint leaves, chopped

2 cloves garlic, very finely diced

Salt and freshly ground pepper, QB

2 tbsp (30 mL) red wine vinegar (optional)

Boil the green beans for 3 to 5 minutes until slightly soft but still a bit crunchy. Drain well, pat dry and put in a mixing bowl. Add olive oil, fresh mint, garlic, salt and pepper, and red wine vinegar if using. Toss gently so the dressing coats all the beans.

Per 4 persone

VERDURE ALLA GRIGLIA
GRILLED VEGETABLES

This is a no-brainer recipe—so simple and yet so delicious.
Pick your favorite vegetables; anything from potatoes to mushrooms to radicchio will work well on the grill.

Unlike roasting, where you preseason the vegetables, grilling is all about what happens after they're cooked, so have some really good olive oil standing by, along with fresh herbs. I like to use a combination of mint, basil and parsley. A lot of recipes call for marinating the vegetables first, but I don't like that: marinated vegetables cause the grill to smoke, and I don't want that smoky flavor. Part of the reason those recipes suggest marinating the vegetables is to prevent sticking, but the key to my method is to make sure the grill is very hot before the vegetables go on.

1 medium eggplant	Salt, QB
1 large zucchini	Chopped fresh mint leaves, QB
1 red pepper	Chopped fresh basil leaves, QB
1 sweet potato	Chopped fresh flat-leaf parsley, QB
Extra-virgin olive oil, QB	

Depending on what vegetables you use, some can go straight on the grill. Some—especially root vegetables like potatoes, sweet potatoes and beets—need to be parboiled. So, clean them, peel them if you like (I peel), put them into cold unsalted water and bring them to a boil. Let them cook for about 10 minutes, until they're somewhat fork-tender—not fully cooked, but softened.

Drain them, and set them aside until they're cool enough to handle. At that point, slice them along with your other vegetables. I often use eggplant, zucchini and sweet potatoes, which I cut into 1/4-inch (5 mm) slices. Roast the red peppers whole. For the method, see page 61.

Heat up your grill until it's hot. Put the vegetable slices on. The trick here is to leave them until they get their grill marks, and not move them around until they're ready to flip, about 5 minutes on each side.

When they're cooked, remove them to a platter and season with good olive oil, salt and fresh herbs. This dish is delicious served immediately, but it will also keep in the fridge for a few days (and become more flavorful).

Per 4–6 persone

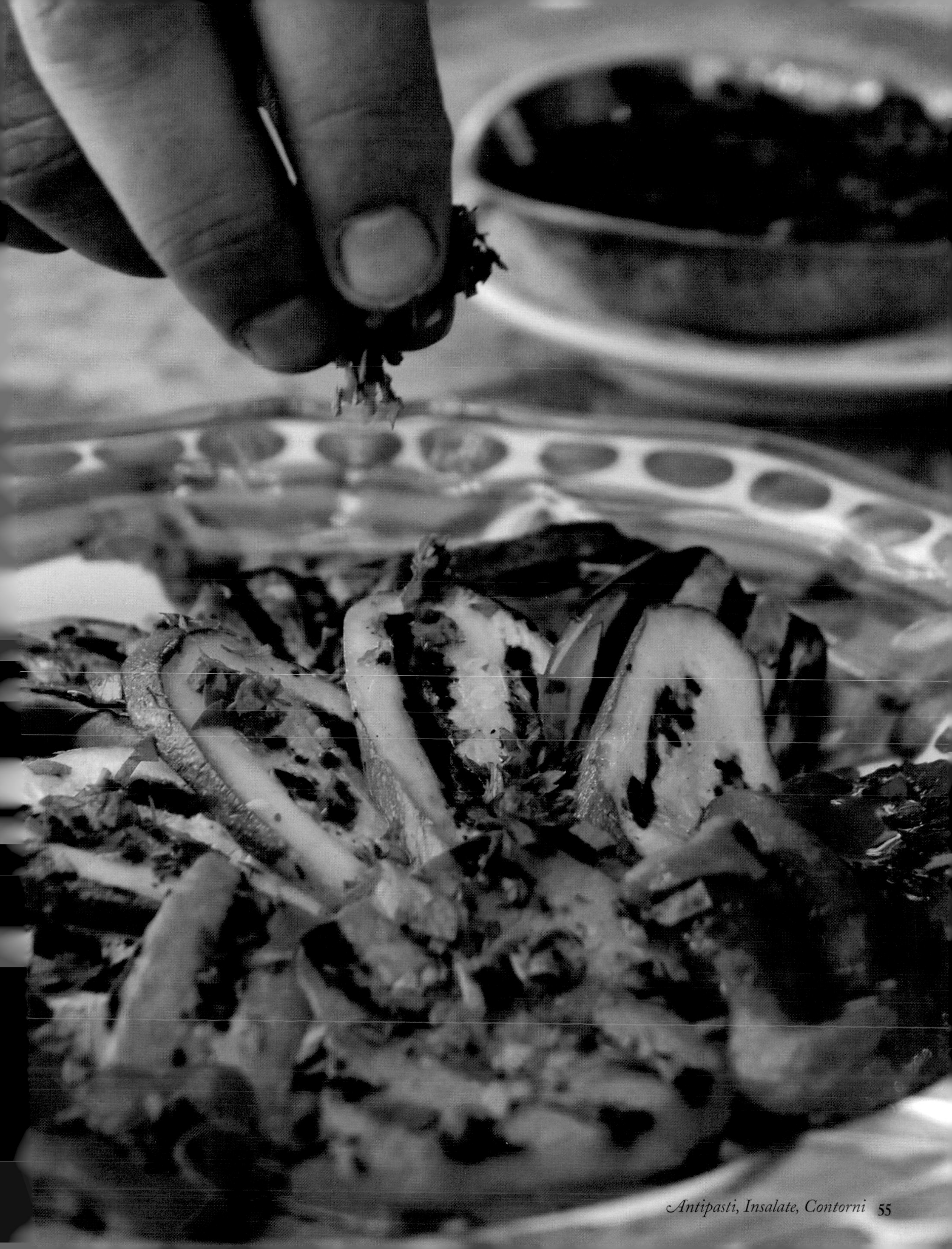

ZUCCHINE E PATATE STUFATE IN PADELLA
STEWED ZUCCHINI AND POTATOES

This is another old-school recipe and is the essence of *cucina povera* or peasant food. I remember my grandmother, who I thought was not a great cook, making these types of dishes all the time when I was a kid. She'd make this in the morning, and it would sit on the stove, for us to eat at dinner. Back then, I looked at this as an unadventurous (i.e., boring) dish. If she really loved me, why couldn't she make a great lasagna with meat sauce and cheese? Lots of cheese!

Well, guess what? I missed the point. Now I love this dish. Like a lot of the classic cucina povera recipes, it's about the simplicity of the ingredients—and the combination of the vegetables is genius.

Now, like my grandmother, I prefer eating this dish at room temperature because, to me, that really lets the flavor of each vegetable settle in. But you can also eat it cold. As well, this is a recipe that you can make when your vegetables are on their last legs.

4 potatoes

4 zucchini

5 tbsp (75 mL) extra-virgin olive oil

2 cloves garlic, crushed

4 zucchini flowers, roughly chopped (optional)

Salt, QB

So for this recipe, peel your potatoes, cut them into chunks, put them in a large pot and cover them with cold water. Bring to a boil and cook until they are mostly tender but not completely cooked, and drain them, reserving 1/2 cup (125 mL) of the cooking liquid.

Wash and slice the zucchini. Bring a pot of water to a boil and drop in the zucchini slices. Because zucchini is a soft vegetable, it will cook in 2 or 3 minutes, so don't overcook! You want the zucchini to still have bite. At that point, drain, reserving about 1/2 cup (125 mL) of the cooking liquid, and set aside.

In a large pan on high heat, heat the olive oil and add the crushed garlic. Add the zucchini flowers and cook until the garlic is brown and the flowers are wilted. Lower the heat to medium, add all your vegetables and the reserved water and stir until everything is fully coated. Add a generous amount of salt, as potatoes tend to absorb it. Put on the lid and cook for about 10 minutes, stirring occasionally. Let the vegetables cool and sit for several hours before serving, so that the flavors come together. Serve at room temperature.

Per 4–6 persone

INVOLTINI DI PEPERONI ARROSTITI
ROLLED ROASTED PEPPERS

Every time I make this for friends or family, they go crazy. It's big impact with no fancy techniques or a cooking diploma necessary! This is another one of those recipes that doesn't require much cooking—it's more about assembling good ingredients, and it's also *quanto basta*, to your taste. The biggest pain in the butt with this recipe is roasting your peppers. The good news is that you can do this a few days in advance, or you can roast them in big batches when they're in season and throw them in the freezer in baggies.

4 red or green peppers

2 tbsp (30 mL) capers

1/2 cup (125 mL) olives of your choice, pitted and halved

1 cup (250 mL) walnuts, shelled

Chopped fresh flat-leaf parsley, QB

1/3 cup (75 mL) bread crumbs

1/3 cup (75 mL) freshly grated Parmigiano-Reggiano cheese

1/3 cup (75 mL) freshly grated pecorino cheese

1/2 cup (125 mL) extra-virgin olive oil

Salt and freshly ground pepper, QB

To roast your peppers in an oven: Put the top rack as high as it goes without having the peppers hit the element. Turn the oven to 400°F (200°C). Put the whole peppers on a sheet pan and slide them in. When the top side blackens and softens, turn them over and cook them until they're charred on all sides. You can also blacken the peppers on a barbecue.

Once the peppers are fully blackened, let them rest in a paper bag for about 15 minutes, so that as they cool down, the steam loosens the skin. Peel off the skin. Halve the peppers, remove and discard the seeds and flatten them out.

For the filling: You can do this in a food processor, or (like me) on a cutting board with a mezzaluna. Finely chop the capers, olives, walnuts and parsley. Put the mixture in a bowl and add the bread crumbs and grated cheeses. Add the olive oil, salt and pepper to taste and combine until the ingredients bind together. If you find that they're not holding together, you can also add a little bit of water. Lay out your pepper halves. Scoop the filling onto the top of each half and roll up. Top with some freshly chopped parsley.

Per 4 persone

INVOLTINI DI MELANZANE E PROVOLA
ROLLED EGGPLANT WITH SMOKED PROVOLONE

Eggplant is a big-time ingredient in Southern Italian cooking. I have to say that when I've spent time in the south of Italy and go back to Tuscany, there are certain dishes I really miss—and many of them have eggplant in them.

So this recipe is Southern-style Italian cooking: it's not complicated and has very few ingredients.

These *involtini* taste fantastic as is. Or you can warm them up, pour my Salsa di Cinque Minuti (page 213) over them, sprinkle with Parmigiano, and all of a sudden you have a quick and easy Parmigiana di melanzane.

2 medium eggplants

Flour, for dredging

2 eggs, beaten

Extra-virgin olive oil, for frying

1–2 balls provola affumicata (or mozzarella or smoked mozzarella cheese)

Thinly slice your eggplant. For this recipe I want the slices almost paper-thin. Dip them into the flour and then into the egg, letting the excess drip off. Heat up your olive oil in a frying pan. You want the oil to be very hot—just before it is about to smoke—otherwise the eggplant will act like a sponge and soak up the oil, and your dish will be very heavy. Fry the eggplant in batches if you have to; don't overcrowd the pan. Once the eggplant is cooked and slightly golden on both sides, remove the slices to a paper towel to absorb any excess oil. Top each slice with a thin slice of provola affumicata and roll. Serve warm or cold. These taste amazing the next day as well, cold from the fridge.

Per 4 persone

PARMIGIANA DI MELANZANE
EGGPLANT PARMIGIANA

In my opinion, this is one of the best representative dishes of Neapolitan cooking. It uses ripe tomatoes, creamy mozzarella cheese and eggplant, which are abundant in Southern Italy. To me, this is happy food.

Now, my dad is from Naples. My mom isn't. But she makes a wicked classic Neapolitan eggplant Parmigiana. Family legend has it that in order to be accepted by my father's family so she could marry my dad, she had to learn from his mother how to make a true eggplant Parmigiana. She clearly passed with flying colors because hers *rules*.

Parmigiana di melanzane is also perfect picnic food. In fact, it was the star player in a Rocco family tradition. My mom would cook it in a big baking tray, cover it with foil and carry it to the car. My dad would put in a gallon of his homemade vino. We'd drive down to Niagara Falls for the day and rendezvous in a parking lot, arriving at about the same time as my cousins. Suddenly, a hundred Roccos would descend on our car, and we'd stand together in the sunshine, eating slabs of the world's best eggplant parm, with the thunder of the falls as a backdrop.

Now, before we get to the good stuff, I want to say this: this dish is what it is. I've seen people try to make this healthy by grilling or baking the eggplant. But it's a lost cause. The flavor that comes from frying is not optional, so don't try to be a hero. The eggplant has to be fried *punto e basta*, as the Italians say, which means "no ifs, ands or buts about it." If you want something light and healthy, eat a carrot.

Continued on page 66

3 tbsp (45 mL) extra-virgin olive oil

2 cloves garlic, crushed

4 cups (1 L) canned peeled plum tomatoes, crushed

Salt, QB

1 bunch fresh basil leaves

4 lb (2 kg) Italian eggplant

2 cups (500 mL) extra-virgin olive oil

2 large balls fior di latte or mozzarella di bufala, shredded

5 oz (150 g) provola affumicata or smoked scamorza cheese, shredded

1 1/2 cups (375 mL) freshly grated Parmigiano-Reggiano cheese

First make a basic tomato sauce: Heat up the 3 tbsp (45 mL) of olive oil, put in some garlic, pour in the crushed tomatoes and cook for 5 minutes. Add salt and a little bit of the basil, ripped up, at the very end. Set aside.

Then the eggplant: Cut it into discs about 1/2 inch (1 cm) thick. Try to make the pieces as close to the same thickness as possible.

Heat up a large frying pan and pour in the 2 cups (500 mL) of olive oil. Let it heat up until it shimmers. This is important: the olive oil has to be hot enough so that the eggplant doesn't absorb the oil, but fries instead, so that the outside becomes crispy and golden. If the eggplant slices are not fully immersed in the olive oil, you may have to turn them over for them to become golden on both sides. As soon as they're done, take them out and set them on some paper towels to soak up the excess oil and salt. Don't layer them.

Preheat the oven to 350°F (180°C).

Ladle a little tomato sauce into a 13- x 9-inch (33 x 23 cm) baking pan and begin as you would for lasagna, making a layer with your cooked eggplant slices. Sprinkle a little of the shredded fior di latte and a little provola over top of the eggplant, and give it a good sprinkling of grated Parmigiano. Finish that first layer with a little tomato sauce and some fresh torn-up basil, and repeat the sequence to make another layer. You can make 2 to 3 layers. Finish with tomato sauce and a layer of cheeses. Bake for 20 minutes, or until the top is crispy and golden. An absolute must: let it rest in the oven with the heat turned off for 1 hour so that it can dry up, and then for at least 1 hour at room temperature before serving.

Per 6–8 persone

CAPONATA SICILIANA
SICILIAN CAPONATA

Caponata is one of the quintessential dishes of Sicily, so you'd think there would be a definitive version. But no such luck. The thing about Italians, food and tradition is that everyone has their own twist, even on the classics, whether it's a family adaptation or a regional spin. And so, with a dish like caponata, there are some basic ingredients, and then the rest is putting your stamp on it.

The staples are eggplant, capers and olives, stewed in a tomato sauce. The dish is both humble and heavenly. That, too, is typical of Italian cooking!

This is one of those heavy Southern dishes, and frankly, it's exactly what bread was made for—to mop up the leftover tomato sauce.

1/2 cup (125 mL) extra-virgin olive oil	3 tbsp (45 mL) capers
2 large eggplants, cubed	1 handful green olives, pitted
1 onion, diced	3 tbsp (45 mL) pine nuts
1 stalk celery, chopped	3–4 tbsp (45–60 mL) red wine vinegar
1 clove garlic, diced	1 can (28 oz/796 mL) peeled plum
Salt, QB	tomatoes, roughly chopped
Chili pepper flakes, QB (optional)	1 bunch fresh flat-leaf parsley, finely
	chopped (optional)

Get a large pan and heat up your olive oil. Add your eggplant, onions, celery and garlic, season with a little salt (and if you want some heat, some chili flakes) and cook on high heat for about 5 minutes, tossing every so often so the vegetables stay fully coated in the oil. When they've softened and are slightly golden, add the capers, olives and pine nuts. Give it all a good stir so that the ingredients mingle nicely. Add the red wine vinegar. Stir and let cook for a few minutes. Then add the tomatoes, bring to a boil, lower the heat and let it simmer for 25 to 30 minutes. Taste for seasonings and add parsley at the very end. Serve warm as a *contorno* or cold as an *antipasto*, but either way, include some nice crusty bread *per fare la scarpetta*—to mop up the beautiful sauce.

Per 4–6 persone

CAPONATA NAPOLETANA
CAPONATA NAPLES STYLE

In Puglia they call this *friselle*, in Campagna, *caponata*; but I call this the ultimate beach food. It's light and screams summer. During one summer holiday in Amalfi, I swear I ate it for lunch for two weeks straight—and then craved it on the plane ride home.

This recipe calls for a hard bread called friselle, which you can find at most Italian grocery stores. The friselle has to be *bagnate*, or quickly plunged into water. For this recipe, give it only a quick soak. You want it to retain its crunch and shape, because it will soak up the liquids in the rest of the ingredients.

2 tomatoes, diced	6 fresh basil leaves, torn
8 anchovies, in olive oil	1 tsp (5 mL) dried oregano (optional)
1 large ball fior di latte or mozzarella cheese, thinly sliced	Salt and freshly ground pepper, QB
1 cup (250 mL) green olives, pitted	1/2 cup (125 mL) extra-virgin olive oil
	4 friselle

In a large bowl, mix all the ingredients except the friselle. Let the mixture rest for about 5 minutes, so that the flavors come together. Take each frisella, dip it quickly into a bowl of water and remove. Put one frisella on each plate and divide the topping equally among them.

Per 4 persone

OLIVE
HARVEST

I had the pleasure of spending time with my friend Faye during the olive harvest. Faye runs her family business, Fattoria Lavacchio, in Tuscany. They make superb organic olive oil and wine, and grow and mill their own grain for bread.

Olives are harvested in the fall, and it's a major celebration in Italy. People start anticipating *l'olio nuovo*—the new olive oil of the season. Some people even take time off their regular jobs to come and pick olives, taking their payment in olive oil. And believe me, handpicking olives is hard work—and labor intensive.

The olives have to be driven to the mill within twenty-four hours of being picked or they'll start to ferment. Each olive squeezes out a few drops of oil—the rest is water and pumice, which is separated out at the mill. One hundred kilos of olives gives you about twelve liters of olive oil. It may seem like a lot of work for little return, but once you've had this oil of the gods, you won't go back to any other.

To be able to go to a *frantoio*, where they press the olives, and dip a piece of bread in that peppery, grassy, buttery, fresh olive oil is, hands down, one of life's true culinary pleasures.

When it's freshly pressed, olive oil is green, and its taste is as rich, complex and intriguing as any wine. The oil has notes of grass or artichokes or herbs or pepper, depending on where the olives were grown. The taste of the new oil mellows with time, so the late fall into Christmas and the New Year is all about making dishes that feature this beautiful new oil.

I use extra-virgin olive oil for everything—including deep-frying. If you've ever had french fries cooked in olive oil, case closed. If anyone tells you they don't like to use it, it's because they don't want to spend the extra money, and that's okay. Yes, extra-virgin olive oil has a lower smoking point, so be careful, but it is worth using. Of course, when you're frying, you don't have to use the best extra-virgin that money can buy.

I always have two bottles on hand, a good one for frying and sautéing, and an amazing one for finishing a dish—whether it's in a salad dressing, or for a pasta or to drizzle on a soup or bruschetta. If you use a really high-quality oil for finishing, you will notice the difference.

I strongly urge you to seek out good olive oil. A lot of great olive oil is made by the wine producers in Italy, like the Planeta, Frescobaldi and Antinori families. You may be able to get some of this oil from the same importer who brings in their wines.

Pinzimonio

Fall is the olive harvest. And in Italy, every meal is another excuse to celebrate the season and use that gorgeous new oil, *l'olio nuovo*.

When I'm in Italy at this time of year, friends and I get together and have a picnic lunch at someone's farmhouse in the cool Tuscan countryside. The highlight is the *pinzimonio* table, which is laid out with fresh, crisp, raw vegetables. Then we pour the season's new olive oil into little individual jars, and offer salt and pepper so everyone can season to their own taste. Some of my favorite vegetables for a pinzimonio are artichokes, fennel, celery, radicchio and leaves of soft lettuces like Boston.

GNUDI DI ZUCCA E L'OLIO NUOVO
BUTTERNUT SQUASH GNUDI WITH FRESH OLIVE OIL

This recipe is much simpler than you might think and absolutely delicious. Gnudi are like big gnocchi. We made this for lunch the afternoon we were picking olives at Fattoria Lavacchio and finished it with olive oil that had been pressed a few days earlier. I would recommend finishing the dish with a drizzle of your best olive oil.

Note: You don't want the ricotta cheese to have too much moisture. If it's runny, put it in a cheesecloth in a colander, over a bowl, so the water drains out. If your dough is too moist, you'll have to add more flour to hold it together, and your gnudi won't be soft and fluffy.

1/2 cup (125 mL) extra-virgin olive oil, preferably l'olio nuovo

1 lb (500 g) butternut squash, peeled, seeded and cut into small cubes

Salt and freshly ground pepper, QB

1 lb (500 g) fresh ricotta cheese

1 1/4 cups (310 mL) freshly grated Parmigiano-Reggiano cheese, plus extra for sprinkling

1 egg

1/2 cup (125 mL) flour (or QB)

Heat half the olive oil in a saucepan on medium heat. Add the butternut squash and the salt and pepper, and sauté until the squash is fork-tender. Now you may ask, why not just boil? Two key reasons: first, you want the squash to pick up the flavor of the olive oil; and second, if you boil the squash, it will retain too much moisture, which does not work well for this dish. When the squash is fork-tender, transfer it to a big mixing bowl. With the back of a fork, work it until it's evenly mashed.

Add the ricotta cheese, 1 cup (250 mL) of the Parmigiano, the egg and about one-third of the flour, and mix everything together. Keep adding flour, a little at a time, until everything is mixed thoroughly and forms a dough.

With your hands, scoop a bit of the mixture and roll it into a ball about the size of a golf ball. Keep going until you've used up all the dough.

Place the gnudi balls in a pot of boiling salted water for about 1 minute or until they float to the surface. Drain and plate.

Drizzle with the l'olio nuovo or the best olive oil you can find, and sprinkle with the remaining Parmigiano.

Per 4–6 persone

FETTUNTA

CANNELLINI BRUSCHETTA

These three beauties are easy: grilled or toasted bread, rubbed with a halved garlic clove, is the base. For the *fettunta*, which literally translates to "oily slice," add a good drizzle of olive oil and salt. The other two are simply smashed cooked white beans and mashed avocado. To finish all of them off, sprinkle salt and pepper, and top with a good drizzle of olive oil. Don't be shy! Remember, the oil is the star ingredient. *È da Dio!*

AVOCADO
BRUSCHETTA

PANZANELLA POVERA
POOR MAN'S PANZANELLA

Leave it to the Italians to figure out how to take stale bread and make it sexy. This is true *cucina povera*. In postwar Italy, when all they had was stale bread and olive oil, this is what they ate. Today on the Amalfi coast, where there's an abundance of good food, this flavorful dried cornbread called *friselle* is still what people eat and love. It's double baked and left to sit until it's rock hard. To serve, the bread is either dipped or soaked in water, then finished with a good drizzle of the best olive oil on hand, some salt and semi-dried oregano. That, with a glass of wine, and I'm very happy. It's a fabulous *merenda*, or snack.

FAVE E PANCETTA
FAVA BEANS AND PANCETTA

So, you're wondering why I want you to make this very unglamorous plate of shriveled-up-looking fava beans. Well, I've been there. When I was a kid, I would resist eating this, convinced—just based on its looks—that there was nothing remotely interesting about this old-man's dish. Ultimately, it was the lure of pancetta that got me to try it. The irony is that now I think its very old-school nature is exactly what makes this dish sexy.

1 lb (500 g) fava beans, shelled	Chili pepper flakes, QB
5 tbsp (75 mL) extra-virgin olive oil	Salt and freshly ground pepper, QB
4 oz (125 g) pancetta, cubed	

Boil the beans in salted water until slightly soft, about 5 minutes. In a frying pan, heat the olive oil until hot, then add pancetta and chili flakes. Cook until the pancetta is slightly golden, then add the drained fava beans, salt and pepper. Cook on high heat for 1 minute or so, then lower to medium-low heat and add 1/2 cup (125 mL) of water. Put the lid on and cook for 10 to 15 minutes, until the favas become soft and the flavors come together.

Per 4 persone

SCAROLA RIPASSATA IN PADELLA
SAUTÉED ESCAROLE

To me, this is total peasant food. It takes me back to when I was a kid and I would watch my relatives pick wild dandelion, endive and chicory in the soccer field behind our house. I still remember my grandmother at the stove, sautéing the wild greens. At the time I was actually embarrassed, thinking we looked like a bunch of poor immigrants. Back then I didn't understand why my relatives wouldn't just go to the store and buy regular vegetables. But now, I think these greens are so delicious and flavorful that I really appreciate why my family went to such great lengths.

This style of sautéing greens also works well with dandelion or rapini.

2 bunches escarole	1 handful Kalamata olives,
5 tbsp (75 mL) extra-virgin olive oil	pitted and halved
4 anchovy fillets, finely chopped	1 handful walnuts, halved
2 cloves garlic, chopped	Salt, QB
Chili pepper flakes, QB	

Give your escarole a good rinse. Cut off the stem end and discard. Give it a rough chop if you like. Bring a pot of water to a rolling boil. Drop in the escarole and cook it until it's tender, about 10 minutes. Drain it in a colander and let cool.

When the escarole is cool enough to handle, pick it up and squeeze out the water; now it's ready to be sautéed.

In a large frying pan, heat up the olive oil. Add anchovies and sauté them until they break down and almost dissolve. Add the garlic, chili flakes, olives and walnuts. Cook until the garlic and walnuts are slightly browned. Add the escarole and a little salt (not too much because the anchovies are salty) and sauté for a few minutes to mix all the flavors and fully cook the escarole.

This dish can be served warm, room temperature or cold. It also tastes great in a panino with slivers of Parmigiano.

You can also use this as the filling for Calzone Scarole (page 148).

Per 4 persone

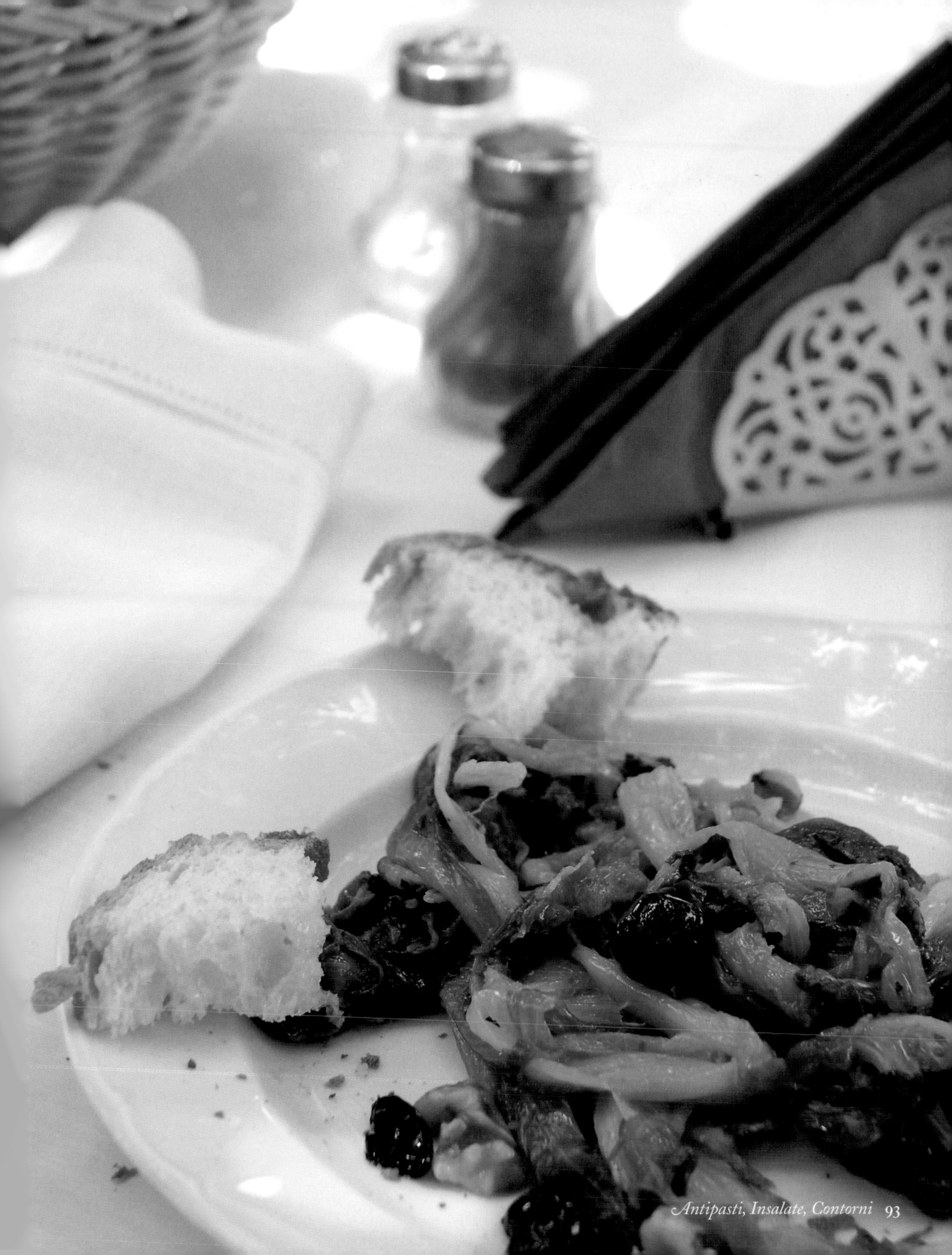

FINOCCHIO IN PADELLA
FRIED FENNEL

I talk a lot about how some of the best cooking is about knowing when to leave well enough alone. This dish is exactly about that. I wasn't sure whether or not I should even put this in the book, because it's so simple that it almost doesn't qualify as a recipe.

But when we were in Italy, I made this one day and the crew tasted it and went crazy. What's in it, they wanted to know. Onions? Garlic? How did I spice it? Did I finish it with a liqueur or grappa? And when I told them the secret, they were blown away.

Sometimes all you need to do is let an ingredient strut its stuff. That's what this dish is about.

Even if you're not crazy about raw fennel, you'll find that this way of cooking brings out another personality: a rich, sweet, caramelized flavor.

I often make this dish when my fennel has been left slightly too long in the fridge, has started to turn a little brown and wouldn't hold up to being served raw.

Extra-virgin olive oil, QB
1 large fennel bulb, sliced, stems and
   fronds discarded

Salt and freshly ground pepper, QB
1/2 cup (125 mL) water

Heat up your olive oil in a large pan. When it's hot, add the fennel and cook until golden. Just before it's done, hit it with some salt and pepper. When the fennel is browned, which means it has some beautiful caramelization going on, that's when you add water. Lower the heat to medium and put the lid on to finish cooking, until the fennel is soft and the liquid has cooked off. What you'll be left with is a gorgeous side for any meat. This tastes delicious hot, at room temperature or cold the next day.

Per 2–4 persone

CAVOLFIORI STUFATI AL POMODORO
THE BEST CAULIFLOWER EVER

To many people, there's nothing very exciting about cauliflower. In fact, it always seems like an old auntie's dish. But when it's cooked a certain way, with some great cheese, I think that it reaches incredible heights. It cooks up to a luxurious silky texture.

Stewed cauliflower is a one-pot meal and so simple that your ten-year-old can make it. You can call him about forty-five minutes before you get home and let him know that "it's time to start cooking, son!" The hardest thing is cutting up the cauliflower, and that's not hard at all. The smaller the pieces, the faster this cooks.

1 large head cauliflower

1 medium white onion

1/2 cup (125 mL) cubed hard cheese, rinds on (optional)

1/4 cup (60 mL) extra-virgin olive oil

1 bunch fresh flat-leaf parsley, chopped

Salt and freshly ground pepper, QB

2 cups (500 mL) tomato purée

1/2 cup (125 mL) water

1/2 cup (125 mL) freshly grated Parmigiano-Reggiano cheese

Cut the cauliflower into small pieces and set aside.

Finely chop up your onion. Now look in your fridge. If you have chunks of tough Parmigiano or cheese that hasn't been properly wrapped, that's perfect! That's exactly what you want. Now is their time to shine. Cube up the tough cheese, rinds and all.

In a fairly large pot, heat up the olive oil and add your onions. Cook until they're translucent. This is your *soffritto*, or your flavor base. Throw in the chopped parsley and all your cauliflower. Give it all a good mix. Add a generous amount of salt and pepper, then add the puréed tomatoes and water. Mix again, lower your heat to medium, put the lid on and let it cook, checking on it every so often, for 40 minutes. Take it off the heat. (I like to give it a fairly rough mix and mash down any large pieces of cauliflower with the back of my spoon.) Now add the pieces of cheese and the grated Parmigiano. Mix it very well and let it rest for 10 to 15 minutes. It will thicken up. This tastes best served warm or at room temperature. Call me an old auntie, but cauliflower alone is one of my absolute favorites.

Per 4 persone

GATEAU DI PATATE
POTATO CAKE

This is like mashed potatoes with an edge. And for a guy like me, who loves potatoes, this has always been a favorite dish. Most people I've served it to love it as well. Not only is it like a giant serving of mashed potatoes, it has a baked crust—like a giant potato croquette without the work. I also look at this dish as a way of using up ingredients in the fridge that have seen better days, like poorly wrapped cheeses, deli meats, etc. It's also great picnic food.

6 potatoes, peeled

4 tbsp (60 mL) extra-virgin olive oil

1 cup (250 mL) diced pancetta
  and/or salami

1 onion, roughly chopped

1 large egg

1/2 cup (125 mL) freshly grated
  pecorino cheese

1/2 cup (125 mL) cubed Parmigiano-
  Reggiano cheese

1/2 cup (125 mL) freshly grated
  Parmigiano-Reggiano cheese

Salt and freshly ground pepper, QB

1 cup (250 mL) bread crumbs

Preheat oven to 400°F (200°C).

Boil potatoes until fork-tender, then drain and let cool. Heat up half the olive oil in a saucepan. Add pancetta and onions. Cook until the onions are golden and the pancetta is crisp.

In a mixing bowl, mash the potatoes. For a creamier texture you can use a potato ricer. Add the egg, the cooked onions and pancetta, all the cheeses and the salt and pepper. Mix well until all the ingredients are evenly combined.

Grease a large baking dish with the remaining olive oil and spread half the bread crumbs over the bottom of the dish. Pour in the potato mixture and spread it evenly, like a cake batter. Sprinkle the rest of the bread crumbs on top. Bake for 20 minutes or until the bread crumbs are golden brown.

This dish tastes delicious warm or at room temperature. In fact, what I sometimes do is make it Sunday morning and then let it sit on top of the stove, so the family can just take slices of it throughout the day. It even tastes good cold, after sitting overnight in the fridge (if there's any left).

Per 4–6 persone

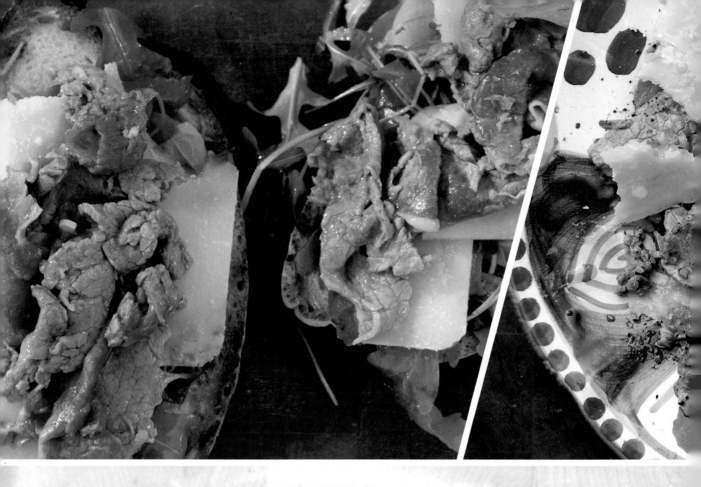

CARPACCIO QUASI COTTO A DUE MODI
HALF-COOKED CARPACCIO TWO WAYS

My sister, Maria, always makes this. It's a reflection of her personality, because she likes stylish food with lots of flavor, but she doesn't have the patience to cook. So this is quick, easy and elegant.

The success of this dish relies on the quality of the ingredients. You want melt-in-your-mouth beef that is good enough to eat raw. Get your butcher to slice it superthin. This is also where you want excellent Parmigiano-Reggiano and your best olive oil. Each component will help make a carpaccio that's out of this world.

It can be served two ways: just on a dish like a classic carpaccio, or on a big *crostone*—toasted or grilled bread.

Extra-virgin olive oil, QB
1 clove garlic, thinly sliced
12 oz (375 g) beef tenderloin
1 bunch arugula, torn

Shavings of Parmigiano-
    Reggiano cheese
Juice of 1 lemon
Salt and freshly ground pepper, QB
4 large slices dense country-style
    bread, grilled or toasted

Pour some olive oil into a pan and heat it up. When it's hot, add the garlic and cook for a few seconds, just enough to flavor the oil. Then put in your beef: you can tear the slices up into smaller pieces or keep them whole. Flash-fry them so that the meat is not fully cooked.

On a serving dish, spread out your arugula and lay the warm, semi-cooked beef right on top. Then, on go the shavings of Parmigiano, freshly squeezed lemon juice, salt and pepper and a really good drizzle of olive oil. I'm never afraid of overdoing it with olive oil, especially with the good stuff, because you can mop it up with the bread.

For something more casual and "snacky," lay your arugula on a piece of toasted or grilled bread and then layer on a few slices of the carpaccio and a shaving of Parmigiano, oil, lemon juice, etc. This is where adding more olive oil makes sense, because the bread is going to soak it up.

Per 4 persone

GAMBERI ROSSI CRUDI MARINATI
MARINATED RAW SHRIMP

I had this at one of my favorite restaurants, da Vittorio, in Porto Palo di Menfi, Sicily. Over the years, Vittorio has become a friend. He's the kind of chef who has no ego. His restaurant is right on the beach, and every morning he walks down to where the fishermen dock with their catch and buys what he wants to cook that day. There are no secrets and no mystery to what he does. He simply gets the best ingredients and doesn't get "cheffy" about how to handle them. He does only enough to bring out the taste of whichever fish he's working with.

Vittorio is a wise man. Shrimp are so sweet and so rich with the flavor of the sea, why would you want to eat them in any way other than their pure state? His delicate marinade slightly cooks the meat and exalts the flavor of the shrimp.

2 lb (1 kg) fresh shrimp	Chili pepper flakes (optional)
Juice of 2 lemons	Extra-virgin olive oil, QB
Salt and freshly ground pepper, QB	Chopped fresh flat-leaf parsley, QB

Shell and clean your shrimp, leaving the heads on. Lay them on a plate. Squeeze fresh lemon juice over them, then sprinkle them with some salt, pepper, chili flakes and a good splash of olive oil. This is a ceviche-style dish that calls for marinating the fish in the lemon juice mixture before serving to partially cook the shrimp. Before serving, sprinkle some fresh parsley over the whole thing.

Note: One of my favorite things to do is suck out the heads of the shrimp. In Italy this is a major compliment to the chef. It's also very flavorful.

Per 4 persone

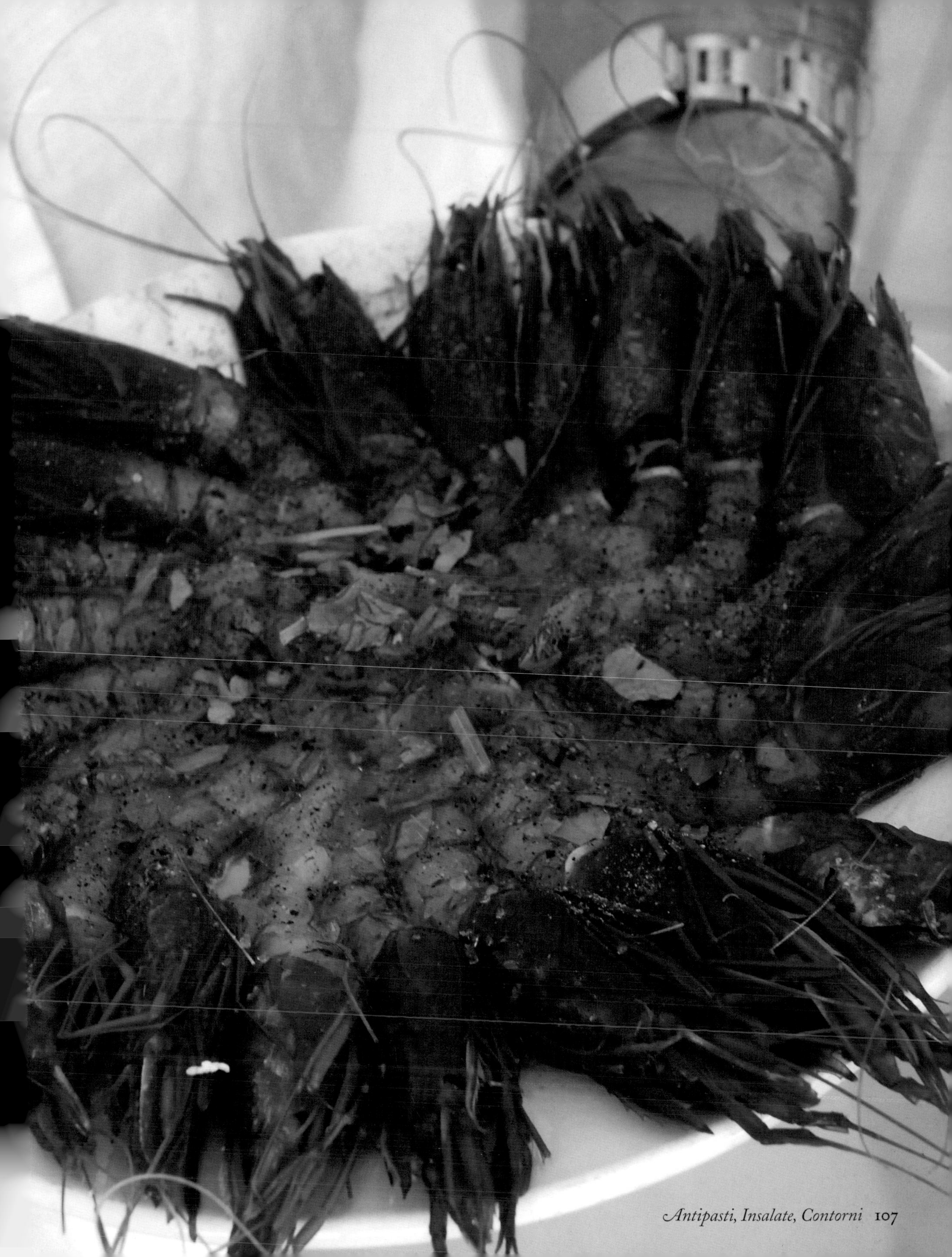

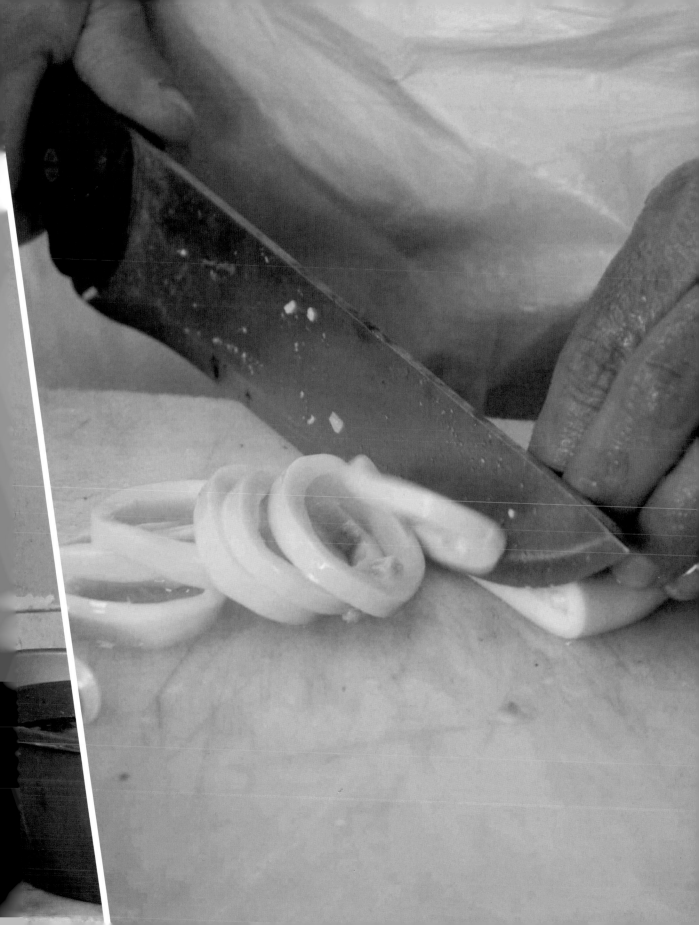

INSALATA DI SEPPIE CON PESTO
CUTTLEFISH SALAD WITH PESTO

I love cuttlefish. To me it tastes like a cross between octopus and squid. I actually prefer it to calamari when used in salads and stews. It's meatier, has a nicer texture and flavor, and is more versatile. In fact, it's much more forgiving than squid. If you overcook squid, it gets rubbery; if you overcook cuttlefish, it just becomes more tender.

Cuttlefish doesn't seem to be used as much in North America as in Italy, but it's easy to find and easy to work with. I'd encourage you to seek it out. These next few cuttlefish dishes are easy to make.

2 lb (1 kg) cuttlefish

Sea salt, QB

1 tbsp (15 mL) Pesto Genovese,
 (page 126)

4 tbsp (60 mL) extra-virgin olive oil

Freshly ground pepper, QB (optional)

Give your cuttlefish a rinse, add to boiling water with fine sea salt and cook for about 15 to 20 minutes or until fork-tender. When it's done, remove it from the water, saving some of the cooking liquid. Let it cool and then slice. Heat up a frying pan. Add a couple of tablespoons (30 mL) of the cooking liquid, the pesto and the cuttlefish slices. Cook for a couple of minutes until the fish is coated with the pesto. Serve it as is or on a bed of sturdy greens like arugula. To finish, drizzle with olive oil and, if you like, fresh black pepper.

Per 4–6 persone

INSALATA DI SEPPIE CON SEDANO E NOCI
CUTTLEFISH, CELERY AND WALNUT SALAD

This is a beautifully refreshing salad for a hot summer day that allows all the ingredients to shine. The crisp celery acts as a perfect bed for the beautifully meaty and tender cuttlefish. The walnuts add some nice earthiness and crunch.

1 1/2 lb (750 g) cuttlefish

3 stalks celery

1/2 cup (125 mL) halved walnuts

4–5 tbsp (60–75 mL) extra-virgin olive oil

Salt and freshly ground pepper, QB

Juice of 1 lemon

Finely chopped fresh flat-leaf parsley, QB

Boil the cuttlefish for 15 to 20 minutes in salted water. There's no science here: when it's fork-tender, it's ready. Drain it and set it aside to cool. You can also put it in the fridge until you're ready to assemble the salad.

Using a mandolin, thinly shred your celery. Put it in an ice bath. The ice will give the celery a nice crisp and cold texture.

When you're ready to serve, cut your cooked cuttlefish into julienne strips and add walnut halves. Season with olive oil and salt and set aside.

Remove the celery from the ice, shake to remove the excess water and dry with a clean cloth or paper towel. Put it in a bowl and season with salt, pepper, lemon juice, a bit of chopped parsley and olive oil. Add the celery to the cuttlefish and walnuts, and toss. Serve immediately.

Per 4 persone

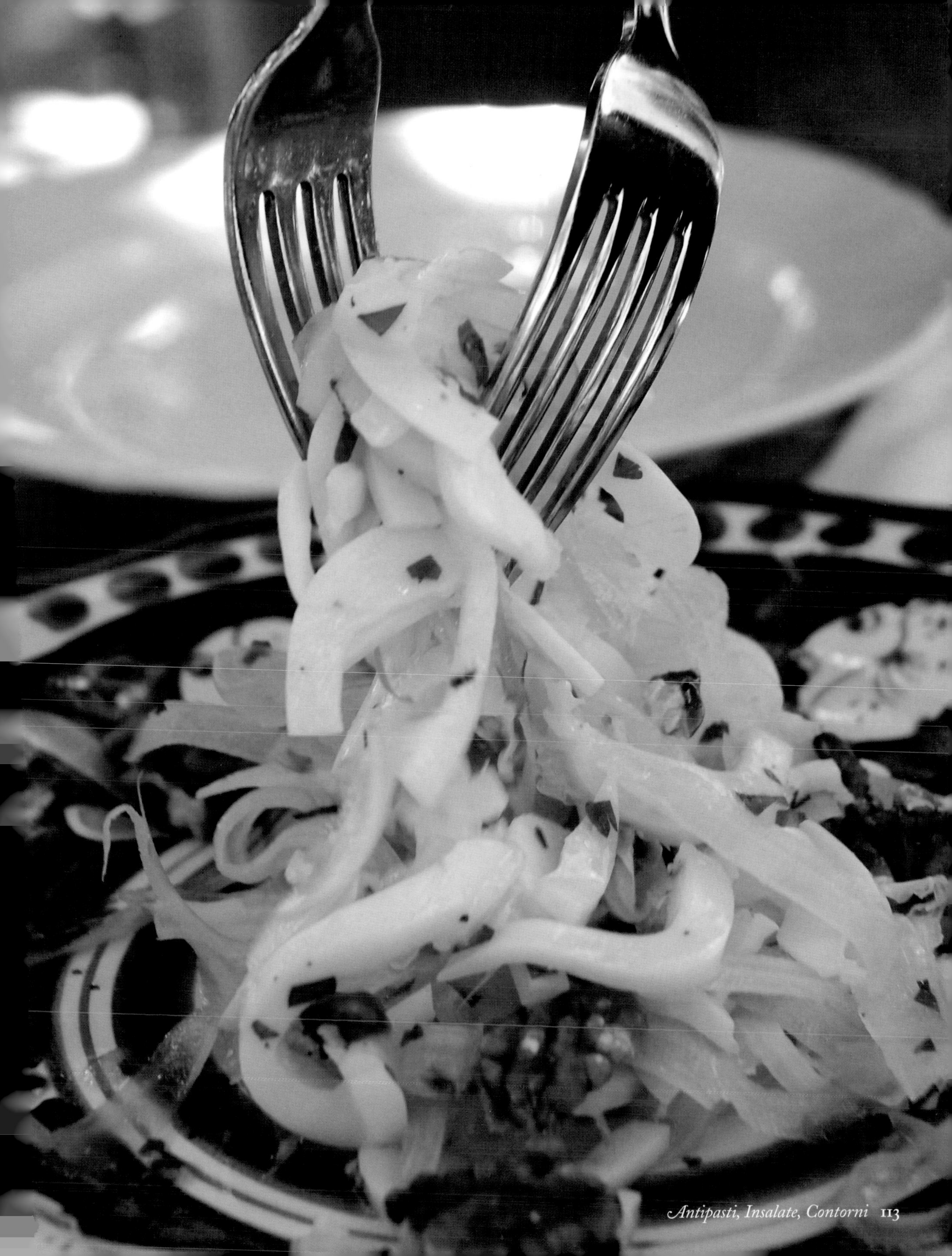

INSALATA DI POLPO CON PATATE E MAIS
COLD OCTOPUS SALAD WITH POTATOES AND CORN

This is essentially a fancied-up version of a basic octopus salad that you'd find in Sicily. There, it would be a boiled octopus, simply dressed *alla salmeriglio*, which is basically an olive oil, lemon and parsley dressing. This version still honors the simplicity of the dish, but throws a modern twist with the addition of potatoes and corn. You can serve this as a salad or as an antipasto. It keeps nicely in the fridge for a few days.

Unless you live by the sea, chances are you'll find your octopus in the frozen-foods section of your supermarket. And then, once it's thawed, you'll have to make sure to clean it. It's not difficult and the rewards are considerable.

1–2 lbs (500 g–1 kg) octopus
2–3 large potatoes
1 bunch fresh flat-leaf parsley,
   finely chopped
1 cup (250 mL) fresh or frozen corn
   kernels, cooked

5 tbsp (75 mL) extra-virgin olive oil
Salt and freshly ground pepper, QB
Juice of 1 lemon

First rinse the octopus well under cold water. Clean the sac, making sure to get rid of any grit. Then flip it over and look for the beak, which is the dark-colored, hard, crusty, shell-like bit. Scoop it out with a paring knife. Now the octopus is good to go. Put it in a large pot with enough cold water to cover it, and bring the water to a boil. No salt is necessary because the octopus will release saltiness as it cooks.

When the water comes to a boil, lower the heat to medium-high and let it continue to cook for about 40 minutes total, or until fork-tender. Again, there's no science here. When the meat is tender, it's ready. Drain it. Let it cool, and then cut it into bite-sized pieces.

At this point, if your great-uncle from Sicily is coming over and you want to go traditional, toss the octopus with olive oil, lemon juice and parsley. But to make a modern version, peel and cut up your potatoes and boil until tender. In a bowl, mix the octopus, potatoes, parsley and corn. Season with a good splash of olive oil, salt and pepper and a squeeze of lemon juice to finish.

Per 6 persone

TONNO CON INSALATA DI CAROTE
TUNA WITH CARROT SALAD

A fresh piece of tuna needs very little. This is a beautiful appetizer. The shredded carrots and mint play a surprisingly strong supporting role—and this is coming from a guy who is not a big carrot fan.

3 large carrots	1/2 cup (125 mL) extra-virgin olive oil
Juice of 1/2 orange	Chili pepper flakes (optional)
Salt, QB	2 lbs (1 kg) sushi-grade tuna fillet
10 fresh mint leaves, finely chopped	Freshly ground pepper, QB
	Sesame seeds (optional)

The tuna is the easy part of this recipe, so you really want to pay attention to the carrots. Wash and peel them and then shred them using a grater.

Add the fresh orange juice, salt, mint, and a drizzle of olive oil and, if you want, a pinch of chili flakes. The chili is optional, but I like a little heat against the sweetness of the orange and the carrots. Mix well and let this marinate for 5 or 10 minutes at room temperature so the flavors can combine. Please make sure you use fresh mint: it plays such an important role in the flavor that this is one time I wouldn't recommend substituting dried for fresh.

Now for your tuna. Start out with the best sushi-grade tuna you can find. Season it with some salt and pepper. If you're using sesame seeds, spread them on a plate and pat both sides of the tuna into them.

Pour some olive oil into a hot skillet, add the tuna and let it cook for a few minutes on each side. It doesn't need much cooking. It should remain pink and raw in the middle. Resist the temptation to turn or move it until you're ready to flip it over.

When it's done, slice it. To serve, arrange the carrot on 6 individual salad plates and top each with a slice of tuna. Finish with a drizzle of your best olive oil.

Per 6 persone

PESTO

Pesto Basics

This is one of my favorite sections of the book. It totally reflects my cooking philosophy and my style in the kitchen. It's about using good ingredients, eyeballing the quantities, tasting as you go and making it your own. In fact, I don't think I've ever made any of these recipes the same way twice.

Pesto is not just the basic basil–pine nut green sauce that most people are familiar with. Its name comes from the Italian *pestare*, which means "to grind or crush," so it basically refers to any sauce that you make using a mortar and pestle, although these days a lot of people like to whip pesto up in a blender or food processor.

I'm a mezzaluna-and-cutting-board guy myself; I prefer that sensual connection with my food. Touching and smelling the ingredients are part of the experience. I also want that rustic texture, not something that looks perfectly uniform and store-bought. But that's my taste. Whatever technique you choose, it's always going to be about the quality of the ingredients.

Pesto will keep a long time in your fridge. Just make sure that your herbs of choice are completely dry, because excess water will spoil the pesto. As well, top it up with olive oil. This will help it keep longer in the fridge. You can also freeze your pesto—it will last a few months.

In general, I serve my pesto over pasta. Because of the intensity, a little goes a long way. Make sure to always reserve a ladleful or so of the pasta cooking water. Always mix your pesto and hot pasta together with the water. This is, of course, QB—you need just a little bit of water to thin out the pesto and evenly dress the pasta.

PESTO GENOVESE/PESTO AMALFITANO
PESTO GENOA STYLE/PESTO AMALFI STYLE

The technique and basic recipe is the same for both of these classic pestos. One is the traditional basil pesto from Genoa that uses pine nuts and basil. The other comes from the Amalfi coast and uses parsley and walnuts. I will often add a spoonful of either to my tomato sauce to make it more intense.

1 bunch fresh basil leaves or flat-leaf parsley	1 cup (250 mL) freshly grated Parmigiano-Reggiano cheese
1/2 cup (125 mL) pine nuts or walnuts	Extra-virgin olive oil, QB
2 cloves garlic	Salt, QB (optional)

Here's the technique: Wash and dry your herb of choice well. Then, lay your herb, nuts and garlic out on a big board. Mulch them with your mezzaluna until the mixture is almost like a paste. Put it in a jar. Add a handful of freshly grated Parmigiano, and pour in olive oil just until the paste is covered. Mix it up. Taste it and add a little more cheese, or if you like, some salt.

Makes approximately 1–2 cups (250–500 mL)

PESTO DI POMODORI SECCHI
SUN-DRIED TOMATO PESTO

This is a beautiful, intense pesto. Sometimes I put a spoonful of this into a regular tomato sauce just to give it extra flavor.

2 cups (500 mL) sun-dried tomatoes	6 anchovy fillets
2 cloves garlic	Extra-virgin olive oil, QB
1 cup (250 mL) pine nuts	Salt (optional)

Chop the sun-dried tomatoes, garlic, pine nuts and anchovies finely with your mezzaluna until the mixture is uniform. Put it all in a jar, and top with olive oil. Stir well. And top it off with more olive oil. Taste it and, if you want, add a pinch of salt.

Makes approximately 2 cups (500 mL)

PESTO DI PREZZEMOLO E LIMONE
PARSLEY AND LEMON PESTO

This is a lovely, light, nut-free summer sauce that can be made on the spot for a quick, delicious and effortless meal. Add a generous amount of this over some perfectly al dente steaming hot spaghetti and *buon appetito*!

2 bunches fresh flat-leaf parsley,
    stems removed
Juice of 2 lemons
Salt and freshly ground pepper, QB

1/2 cup (125 mL) freshly grated
    Parmigiano-Reggiano cheese
Extra-virgin olive oil, QB

Wash and dry the parsley well. Place it on a cutting board and with a mezzaluna chop finely. Place in a jar and add freshly squeezed lemon juice. Add salt, pepper, Parmigiano and olive oil. Mix well.

Makes approximately 1–2 cups (250–500 mL)

PESTO D'OLIVA
OLIVE PESTO

Most people think of tapenade when they think of olive paste, but this olive pesto makes a terrific sauce for your pasta. Pecorino works better than Parmigiano for this recipe because the ingredients in this pesto are very bold and you need a cheese that will stand up to those flavors.

1 cup (250 mL) almonds
2 cups (500 mL) black and green olives,
    pitted
1 fresh chili pepper

1 handful fresh basil leaves
1/2 cup (125 mL) freshly grated pecorino
    cheese
Extra-virgin olive oil, QB

Toast your almonds in a dry frying pan for about 5 minutes, or until they turn slightly brown. On a cutting board with your mezzaluna, chop your olives, almonds, chili pepper and basil until you get a nice mulch. Put it all in a jar and add the pecorino. Pour in enough olive oil to cover and mix well.

Makes approximately 2–3 cups (500–750 mL)

Sun-Dried Tomatoes

Traveling through the town of Pachino, on the southern tip of Sicily, you will see fields of sun-dried tomatoes along the country roads.

Drying tomatoes in the sun is easy to do if you live in southern Italy, where it's reliably dry and sunny for days at a time and where the temperatures can hit 95°F (35°C). There, you cut your tomatoes in half and lay them out on mesh racks so that the heat circulates and dries them thoroughly. In Sicily, cherry tomatoes dry in about three days.

If you live in colder climates, you may not have the Sicilian sunshine, but you can dry tomatoes in your oven. The good news is that it doesn't take three days.

On a baking sheet, lay out your tomatoes and bake in a preheated oven at 400°F (200°C).

You don't need to add any salt, other seasonings or olive oil. It's all about the quality of the tomatoes. Check on them every so often, but they should be done in about 90 minutes. I like mine to be semi-dried, so that I still get the intense flavor but they aren't tough like cardboard.

PESTO DI PEPERONCINO DI ZIO ERNESTO
UNCLE ERNIE'S CHILI PESTO

If you love chili or chili oil, this is going to be your new favorite pesto.

This sauce, or a variation on it, was my Uncle Ernesto's specialty. I love the way the heat of the chili contrasts with the sweetness and depth of flavor of the sun-dried tomatoes and basil. What you end up with is a beautiful sweet sauce with a kick afterwards. And you control the kick. So, if you want it super spicy, keep some of the seeds in the peppers. If you want it sweeter, use more basil and sun-dried tomatoes. You can use this pesto as a spread for sandwiches, on pizzas or—my favorite—spooned onto already sauced pasta, whenever you want extra heat.

So here's the deal: my Uncle Ernie told me only the ingredients, no amounts, which makes this totally QB. And he wasn't holding back or giving attitude. This is just how it goes in my family. I've given you some quantities, but frankly, as with all of these pestos, just make them your own, as I did with this one.

1 bunch fresh basil leaves	1 cup (250 mL) sun-dried tomatoes
1 cup (250 mL) fresh chili peppers	1/2 cup (125 mL) extra-virgin olive oil
2 cloves garlic	(or QB)

Here's what you do: Grab your basil, wash it and pat it dry. Lay it out on a big cutting board with the chili peppers, garlic and sun-dried tomatoes (I recommend that you don't use the ones packaged in oil; you don't know what kind of oil it is) and, with your mezzaluna, chop away. You want to create a mulch that incorporates all the ingredients. I put my sauce into washed jam jars and pour good olive oil in until the pesto is completely covered. Give it a good stir, top with more olive oil and you're good to go. Store it in your fridge, but don't expect it to last long, especially if you like spice.

SALSA VERDE

This rich, bright-tasting sauce is less compact than a conventional pesto sauce. It's usually served with meat and, in my world, as part of a *bollito* (page 165). There are no nuts and no cheese. It gets its phenomenal flavor from the combination of anchovies and capers. This also goes well with grilled fish or calamari.

1 large bunch fresh flat-leaf parsley, stems removed
3 1/2 oz (100 g) capers
6–8 anchovy fillets
Salt and freshly ground pepper, QB
Juice of 1–2 lemons
Extra-virgin olive oil, QB

Place parsley, capers and anchovies on a cutting board.

With a mezzaluna, finely chop the ingredients.

Place in jar. Add salt and pepper, freshly squeezed lemon juice and olive oil. Mix well and top with more olive oil.

Makes approximately 1 cup (250 mL)

One of my earliest memories in Italy is going to have pizza late at night in Naples. We kids would always have it with Fanta, while the adults would have theirs with beer. Italians are interesting. They drink wine with almost everything, but when it comes to one of the iconic Italian dishes, it seems to me that they prefer something crisp or bubbly—a beer or a soft drink—to vino.

In many *pizzerie* in Naples, where pizza was invented, you will be offered only two kinds: Margherita and Marinara, and that's it.

The belief is that pizza should be simple: great dough and only a few toppings. Those of you who have had a pizza in Naples, with the charred bottom, slightly chewy dough and moderate toppings, know what I mean.

When it comes to pizza, if you're focused on the toppings, then you're putting the cart before the horse. The real key to the dish is the quality of the crust.

I am not a food snob, nor am I a pizza snob, *but* I think that it's worth learning how to make your own pizza dough. It's not as complicated as you might imagine, and you'll thank me for it. And if you're a real pizza freak, invest in a wood-burning oven, which produces a pizza that you can't really replicate in any other kind of oven, and makes for great outdoor dining.

Having said all of that, I will also say that in life, time is not always on your side. And if your desire for pizza strikes when you don't have time to let your dough rise and you haven't built your wood-burning oven yet, it's worth sourcing out a place that makes a great pizza dough, one that is made as simply as possible. And for the regular oven, it's worth investing in a pizza stone. Make sure your oven and the pizza stone are heated before you put the dough in.

L'IMPASTO PER LA PIZZA
PIZZA DOUGH

As the saying goes: order a man a pizza and he'll eat for a day; teach him how to make his own terrific dough and he'll impress everyone for life.

> 2 cubes (each 1/4 oz/7g) fresh yeast or 2 1/2 tsp (12 mL) active dry yeast
> 1 1/2 cups (375 mL) lukewarm water
> 4 cups (1 L) flour
> 1 tsp (5 mL) salt
> 1/2 cup (125 mL) white wine, at room temperature
> 2 tbsp (30 mL) extra-virgin olive oil

Stir the yeast into the lukewarm water and let it dissolve completely. (If you're using cubes, you'll need to break them up.) Allow to rest 10 minutes until it starts to bubble up.

Pour the flour and salt onto a smooth work surface and create a well in the middle of the flour.

Now, to make the dough, pour your water and yeast mixture into the middle of the well, a little at a time, and, using a fork, start mixing by drawing some of the flour from the inner edge of the well into the water. Keep doing this until all the flour has been drawn in. Once the yeast mixture is incorporated, add the wine and then the olive oil, working the mixture with your hands until it is well combined and you can create a ball.

Knead the dough by rolling it back and forth, stretching it out with one hand and rolling it back with the other. Continue for about 5 minutes or until the dough is smooth and has an almost spongy texture. Divide the dough into 6 equal parts (one for each pizza), put a damp dish towel over them and leave them out at room temperature for about 1 hour. The dough will double in size. Punch it down, and now you're ready to roll it out and make your pizzas (or freeze for future use). Was that so hard?

Per 6 pizze (9–10 inch)

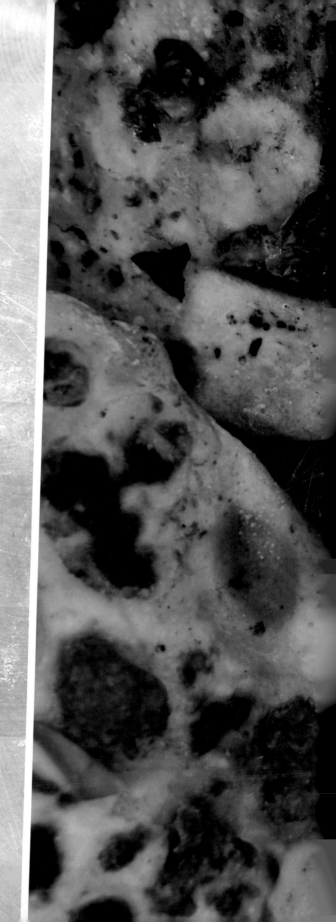

These next pizzas are simple and are staples at our Sunday pizza parties. Trust me: if your dough is flavorful and your ingredients are good, you don't need to slop extra toppings on.

A few things you need to know when rolling out your pizzas: Work on a clean, dry surface that's dusted with a little flour. This is where a marble slab will come in handy if you have one. With the heel of your hand, flatten the ball of dough into a mini-sphere. Roll it out with a rolling pin and then turn the pizza to the unrolled side. Keep rolling and turning until the pizza has been rolled out flat to the size and thickness that you want. If you're using a regular oven, put the dough onto a pizza pan, either lightly greased or lined with parchment paper, or on a (preheated) pizza stone. Now it's all about your toppings. First thing: preheat your oven to 450°F (230°C). These pizzas should bake in 10 to 12 minutes. If you're using a wood-burning oven, you're looking at 2 to 3 minutes. The following pages feature some of my favorites.

PIZZA PATATE E ROSMARINO
POTATO AND ROSEMARY PIZZA

This potato pizza is *so* flavorful. The slices of potato and the rosemary work perfectly together. If you've never had this, it will quickly become one of your favorites.

Dough for 1 pizza (page 141)

1 potato, thinly sliced

1 medium onion, thinly sliced

1 sprig fresh rosemary, stem removed

Salt, QB

Extra-virgin olive oil, for drizzling, QB

Roll out your dough. Top with potato and onion slices and sprinkle the rosemary evenly over them. Add salt and a good drizzle of olive oil. Bake for 2 to 3 minutes in a wood-burning oven or 10 to 12 minutes at 450°F (230°C) in a regular oven. Drizzle a little olive oil onto the pizza as soon as it comes out of the oven.

PIZZA CIPOLLE E PEPERONCINI
ONION AND CHILI PIZZA

I think of this pizza as a really tasty bread. I make it when I'm serving great cheeses, salami and prosciutto.

Dough for 1 pizza (page 141)

1 white onion, thinly sliced

1 fresh chili pepper, sliced

Extra-virgin olive oil, QB

Salt and freshly ground pepper, QB

Roll out your dough. Top with the onion slices, chili pepper, a good drizzle of olive oil, salt and pepper. Bake for 2 to 3 minutes in a wood-burning oven or 10 to 12 minutes at 450°F (230°C) in a regular oven. I always finish the pizza with a good drizzle of olive oil when it comes out of the oven.

PIZZA SALSICCIA E SCAMORZA
SAUSAGE AND SCAMORZA PIZZA

I love the combination of smoky scamorza and sausage. With essentially only two ingredients, this pizza is not very complicated—but incredibly flavorful.

Dough for 1 pizza (page 141)

8 oz (250 g) pork sausage

2 oz (60 g) smoked scamorza cheese, thinly sliced

Extra-virgin olive oil, QB

Salt, QB

Roll out your dough. Take the casing off the sausage and crumble the meat over the dough. Spread out the slices of scamorza, drizzle with olive oil, sprinkle on some salt and bake for 2 to 3 minutes in a wood-burning oven or 10 to 12 minutes at 450°F (230°C) in a regular oven.

PIZZA POMODORI E PARMIGIANO
TOMATO AND PARMIGIANO PIZZA

I can't have a pizza party without a pizza that features tomatoes. This is simple. Use the sweetest cherry tomatoes available.

Dough for 1 pizza (page 141)

5–7 cherry tomatoes, halved

Freshly grated Parmigiano-Reggiano cheese, QB

Fresh basil leaves, torn, QB

Salt, QB

Extra-virgin olive oil, QB

Roll out your dough. Squeeze the halved cherry tomatoes, letting the juices fall onto the dough, and then spread out the crushed tomatoes. Grate Parmigiano over it, then add some ripped-up basil leaves and salt to taste. Drizzle it with a little olive oil and bake for 2 to 3 minutes in a wood-burning oven or 10 to 12 minutes at 450°F (230°C) in a regular oven. Give it another drizzle when it comes out of the oven.

Pizza calzone tre modi
Calzone three ways

What's the difference between making a regular flat pizza and a folded pizza? Hard for me to answer, because when I eat my pizza, I usually fold it, so to me all pizzas are effectively folded pizzas. The message to you is this: if you've made a pizza, and if you can pinch, then you can easily make one of these babies.

CALZONE SCAROLE
ESCAROLE CALZONE

This is probably my favorite stuffed pizza. When I made this for my Tuscan television crew they initially snubbed it, mocking my Southern Napolitano roots. They all said this stuffing made no sense. Maybe they weren't impressed that I was using escarole that was past its prime. Who knows? Damned Tuscans. What do they know about food? But when this came out of the oven, they rushed to taste it and wanted me to make more.

Even if this used just escarole, you'd have a delicious dish. But then you add the raisins, olives and pine nuts, and it's like an explosion of flavor in every bite. And if you doubt it, there's a television crew wandering around Tuscany with a new appreciation for Neapolitan ingenuity.

1 bunch escarole	1 cup (250 mL) olives
4 tbsp (60 mL) extra-virgin olive oil	1/2 cup (125 mL) raisins
2 cloves garlic, crushed	Kosher salt, QB
Chili pepper flakes, QB	Dough for 1 pizza (page 141)
2 anchovy fillets	Extra-virgin olive oil, for brushing, QB
1/2 cup (125 mL) pine nuts	3 anchovy fillets, for topping (optional)

Give your escarole a good rinse. Cut off the stem end and discard. Cook the escarole in boiling water for about 10 minutes, then drain. When it's cool enough to handle, squeeze out the excess water.

Heat up a frying pan. Add olive oil, garlic, chili flakes and 2 anchovies. Let that cook for a few minutes until the anchovies start to dissolve. Add your pine nuts, olives and raisins. Cook a few minutes more until the pine nuts toast and become fragrant. Add the escarole and sauté for a few minutes to mix all the flavors. Add a bit of salt, but be careful because the anchovies and olives are already salty, so don't overdo it. Roll out your dough. Lay the topping on half of the dough, leaving a 1/2-inch (1 cm) border. Fold the plain side over the side with toppings, and pinch the edges together to close the calzone. Brush with olive oil. Sprinkle with a touch of kosher salt. Lay the 3 additional anchovies on top. Bake for 3 to 5 minutes in a wood-burning oven or 10 to 12 minutes at 450°F (230°C) in a regular oven. Let it stand for a few minutes, or better yet, let it cool to room temperature.

CALZONE SPINACI E FONTINA
SPINACH AND FONTINA CALZONE

Spinach and fontina are a beautiful combination.

1 bunch spinach, chopped
3 tbsp (45 mL) extra-virgin olive oil
2 cloves garlic, crushed
Chili pepper flakes, QB

Kosher salt, QB
2 oz (60 g) fontina cheese, sliced
Dough for 1 pizza (page 141)
Extra-virgin olive oil, for brushing, QB

Sauté your spinach in a pan with the olive oil, garlic and chili flakes. Add a little bit of salt, remove from the heat and let the spinach cool. Roll out your dough as you would for a regular pizza. Spread the spinach and fontina on half of the dough, leaving about a 1-inch (2.5 cm) border. Fold the plain side over the side with toppings. Pinch the edges together to close the calzone. Brush with olive oil and sprinkle with a touch of kosher salt. Bake for 3 to 5 minutes in a wood-burning oven or 10 to 12 minutes at 450°F (230°C) in a regular oven. When it comes out, brush the top again with a little bit of olive oil. Let it sit for a few minutes before serving.

CALZONE PROSCIUTTO COTTO E SCAMORZA
HAM AND SCAMORZA CALZONE

This is more in line with what my Tuscan crew was used to having. Delicious.

Dough for 1 pizza (page 141)
4 oz (125 g) prosciutto cotto, sliced
2 oz (60 g) smoked scamorza cheese,
   thinly sliced

5–7 sun-dried tomatoes, chopped
Extra-virgin olive oil, for brushing, QB
Kosher salt, QB

Roll out your dough. Spread the prosciutto cotto, scamorza and sun-dried tomatoes over half of the dough, leaving a 1-inch (2.5 cm) border. Fold the plain side over and pinch the edges together to close the calzone. Lightly brush the dough with olive oil and sprinkle with kosher salt. Bake for 3 to 5 minutes in a wood-burning oven or 10 to 12 minutes at 450°F (230°C) in a regular oven. Remove it from the oven and let it sit to cool. Eat warm or at room temperature.

FOCACCIA ALLA PIASTRA
GRILLED FOCACCIA SANDWICH

At your next barbecue, try grilling your dough. It's remarkably easy and the dough cooks well on top of the grill. What's nice about doing this on the barbecue is that the outside of the dough becomes a little crispier. But you can also bake this in the oven like a regular pizza.

Dough for 1 pizza (page 141)

1 small bunch arugula, torn

Juice of 1/2 lemon

Extra-virgin olive oil, QB

Salt, QB

4–5 slices prosciutto, thinly sliced

Shavings of Parmigiano-Reggiano
   cheese, QB

Preheat the barbecue until very hot. Turn the burners down to a low flame and lay the rolled dough on the grill. Close the lid and don't touch for a couple of minutes. When the dough is ready to flip, the underside will be crisp and lightly grill-marked. Flip and cook the other side in the same manner, about three minutes more.

In a bowl, mix arugula with freshly squeezed lemon juice, olive oil and salt. Spread the mixture on your grilled dough, then layer on the prosciutto and shavings of Parmigiano. Fold the focaccia and serve like a sandwich.

Per 1 persona

PIZZA FRITTA

This snack will blow your mind. It's probably my favorite in this entire section—which is really saying something, because I love all these pizzas—and it's super easy to make. Okay, so it's fried pizza dough, but trust me, it's worth it. When you fry the dough, it changes the whole taste and texture of the pizza: it's soft, fluffy and chewy, and slightly crispy at the same time, if you can wrap your mind around that. And frying always makes whatever dough you have taste that much better, so you can use store-bought dough for this and still achieve greatness. Just make sure that the oil is really hot (it will shimmer) before you put the pizzas in.

There are three ingredients here—the fresh tomato sauce, the pizza and the pecorino—and they all hold their own, providing contrast and complementing each other. This tomato sauce is perfect for pizza. Because you don't start it off with a soffritto—fried or sautéed garlic—the sauce is lighter and fresher tasting, which is exactly what you want for pizza fritta.

Fresh Tomato Pizza Sauce:

1 can (28 oz/796 mL) peeled plum
   tomatoes, crushed

Salt, QB

2 cloves garlic, cut in large chunks

3 tbsp (45 mL) extra-virgin olive oil

Dough for 3 pizzas (page 141)

Freshly grated sharp pecorino cheese, QB

Fresh basil leaves, QB

Extra-virgin olive oil, for frying

In a saucepan, bring the crushed tomatoes, salt, garlic and olive oil to a light boil. Taste and adjust for seasonings. Turn off the heat and let it rest. Discard the garlic.

For your dough:

Cut it into strips. Then, with your hands, stretch and shape the strips into little discs about the size of your hand.

Heat up about 1 to 2 inches (2.5 to 5 cm) of olive oil in a deep sauté pan. Let it get nice and hot.

Gently lay the pizzas in the hot oil. Don't overcrowd the pan. Fry the pizzas until they become light and fluffy and airy. They'll puff while you're watching them. Flip them over and cook the other side until they're slightly golden, then remove to a plate lined with paper towels. Spoon your fresh tomato sauce over the pizzas. Sprinkle some sharp pecorino onto them and top with some basil.

Per 4–6 persone

Pizza Dolce

Broken down to its basics, a pizza is a beautiful dough that plays host to a variety of flavors and textures. So why not sweet?

I COCCOLI

This very Tuscan treat is easy to make. It's what bakers do with the leftover bits of dough from the bread and pizza; they fry it up and serve it as a snack. *I toscani* have it two ways: the savory way is with thin slices of prosciutto and creamy stracchino cheese, and the sweet version is salted and then drizzled with honey. I even like it plain, just salted, hot out of the fryer.

Flour, for dusting
Dough for 3 pizzas (page 141)
Extra-virgin olive oil, for frying
Salt, QB
Honey, for drizzling, QB

Sprinkle flour on a worktable. Roll out the dough to about a 1/4-inch (5 mm) thickness.

Cut the dough into small squares like ravioli.

Pour at least 1 inch (2.5 mm) of olive oil into a deep saucepan. Gently place the squares in the hot oil, a few at a time. Fry until they have puffed up and are golden, then flip and cook on the other side.

Remove with a slotted spoon and transfer to a plate lined with paper towels. Sprinkle with salt while hot. Then drizzle with honey and serve.

Per 6–8 persone

CALZONE MASCARPONE E NUTELLA
MASCARPONE AND NUTELLA CALZONE

To me, Nutella ranks up there with Sophia Loren, Vespa and Ferrari as an iconic Italian brand. It's enough to convince you that there is a heaven. I think you could spread it on a shoe and the shoe would taste amazing. So imagine what happens when you put Nutella together with creamy mascarpone and bake it inside of a delicious basic dough. Yes, you could end the night ten pounds heavier, but this calzone is worth the risk.

Dough for 1 pizza (page 141)
3 tbsp (45 mL) mascarpone cheese (or QB)
3 tbsp (45 mL) Nutella (or QB)
Extra-virgin olive oil, for brushing, QB
Kosher salt, QB

Roll out your dough. Spread the mascarpone cheese on one half of the dough and the Nutella on the other half.

Fold the Nutella side over the mascarpone side (or the other way around) and pinch the edges together.

Lightly brush the dough with olive oil and sprinkle with salt. The sprinkle of salt is important here. Wait until you get a hit of salt against the sweetness of Nutella!

Bake for 3 to 5 minutes in a wood-burning oven or 10 to 12 minutes at 450°F (230°C) in a regular oven.

Per 1–2 persone

SCHIACCIATA CON L'UVA
GRAPE PIZZA

For me, this dish conjures up memories of the fall grape harvest in Italy. It's traditionally made when the Sangiovese grapes are in season. This is a very simple recipe, with really only four ingredients: pizza dough (and you can use store-bought for this), grapes, sugar and rosemary. The grapes are crushed so they flavor the dough; the sugar is sprinkled over and caramelizes in the oven. To some people, the idea of putting a woodsy herb like rosemary with grapes and sugar seems odd, but its flavor is exactly what this dish needs to bring it all together. You can either put the ingredients on top of a single layer of dough or do what they do in Tuscany—fold your dough in half and add a second layer of grapes, sugar and rosemary for double the goodness. This recipe is for the Tuscan version.

Dough for 3 pizzas (page 141)
1 bunch Concord or Sangiovese grapes
1 cup (250 mL) sugar
2 sprigs fresh rosemary
3 tbsp (45 mL) extra-virgin olive oil

Preheat oven to 400°F (200°C). Grease a baking sheet with olive oil. Stretch and flatten out the dough until it's about 1/4-inch (5 mm) thick. Lay the dough over the baking sheet so that half of it is on and the other half is off.

On the half that's on the sheet, spread half the grapes and press down on them with your hands so that the juices run into the dough. Sprinkle half the sugar over the grapes. Then hold a rosemary sprig upside down over the pizza, run your fingers down over it so the leaves are released over the dough, and discard the stem. Finish the layer by drizzling half of the olive oil evenly over the whole thing. Fold the plain flap of dough over this finished layer and pinch the edges together. Repeat the process with the remaining grapes, sugar, rosemary and olive oil on the top layer.

Bake for 15 to 20 minutes, or until the pizza is cooked and golden.

Per 6–8 persone

PIZZA MELE E GORGONZOLA
APPLE AND GORGONZOLA PIZZA

To me, apple, Gorgonzola, walnuts and honey are a perfect combination. So imagine baking them on a beautiful dough.

Dough for 1 pizza (page 141)
1 apple, peeled, cored and sliced
2 oz (60 g) Gorgonzola cheese, crumbled
1/2 cup (125 mL) walnuts, halved
Honey, for drizzling, QB

Stretch and roll out dough. Top with apples, Gorgonzola and walnuts, then drizzle with honey. Bake for 3 to 5 minutes in a wood-burning oven or 10 to 12 minutes at 450°F (230°C) in a regular oven.

PIZZA UVA E PIGNOLI
PIZZA WITH GRAPES AND PINE NUTS

I love the mix of fruit and nuts on a delicious pizza dough.

Dough for 1 pizza (page 141)
10 grapes, halved
1/4 cup (60 mL) pine nuts
Sugar, for sprinkling, QB

Stretch and roll out the dough. Place the grapes on the dough, cut side down. Add pine nuts and sprinkle with sugar. Bake for 2 to 3 minutes in a wood-burning oven or 10 to 12 minutes at 450°F (230°C) in a regular oven.

STREET LIFE

Maybe it's because of Italy's weather or because apartments are small, but there's always something happening on the street. Go to any city on a Sunday afternoon after lunch, or *pranzo*, and the streets will be packed with locals going for their afternoon stroll or for the post-meal coffee or gelato. In Italy, everyone comes out to walk, to visit, to argue about politics or soccer, to see and be seen. It's part of the Italian lifestyle.

BOLLITO CON SALSA VERDE E PEPERONCINO
BOLLITO WITH SALSA VERDE AND CHILI PESTO

This is a joke among my friends. I absolutely cannot go into *il centro di Firenze* without having lunch or a snack from one of my favorite *bollito* carts. The bollito is the hot dog or fast food of Florence. The carts sell three kinds of meat: *lampredotto* and *trippa*, which are both tripe stewed in tomato sauce and served in a bun; and bollito, which is a long-simmered meat served in the same way.

You can get a little glass of wine to go along with them, which I'd recommend. And then you either stand around and talk to the locals or grab a spot on the steps of the Duomo and people watch. What's great is that the bollito carts are in piazzas, so it's not just about the food but also the atmosphere, the art, the architecture, the hustle and bustle.

My favorite is Roberto Marchetti's L'Antico Trippaio in Piazza dei Cimatori, tucked into the side streets between Piazza della Signoria and the Duomo.

8 cups (2 L) water	1 onion, quartered
2 lb (1 kg) stewing beef	1 clove garlic, crushed
2 carrots, halved	Salsa Verde (page 135)
2 stalks celery, halved	Pesto di Peperoncino (page 132)

Bring the water to a boil in a large pot. Add your beef, carrots, celery, onion and garlic. Cook for 3 hours on a simmer, or until the meat becomes fall-apart tender, and then take it out of the pot.

Slice or shred the boiled meat and serve with the salsa verde and chili pesto. You can eat the bollito either on its own or on a bun, as a sandwich.

Per 6–8 persone

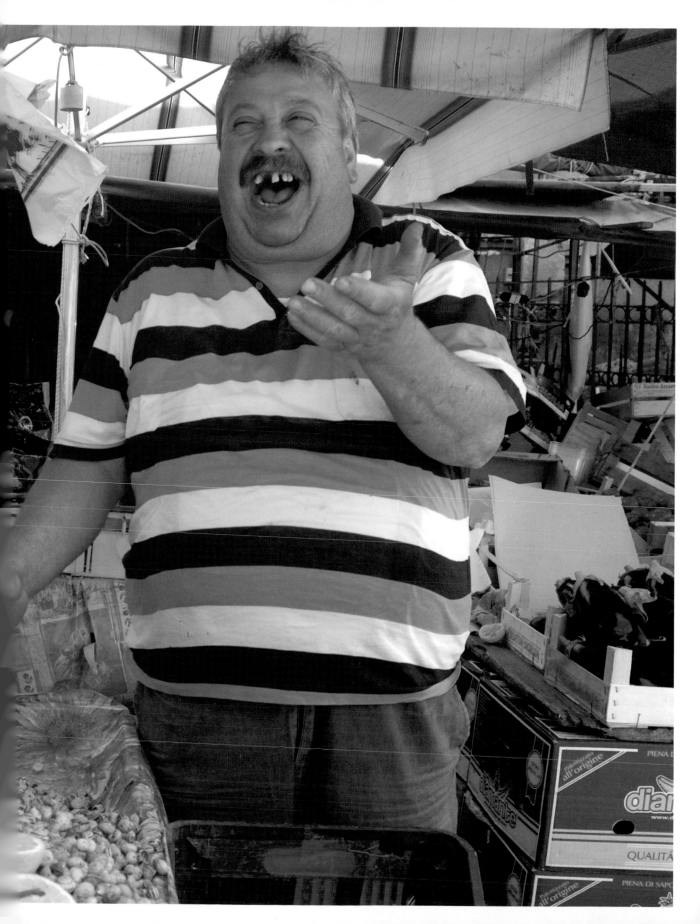

Primi

In a traditional Italian meal, *il primo* is the first course, after the *antipasti*. It's usually a *zuppa*, *pasta* or *risotto*.

Zuppa

I grew up in a cold country, where hot, hearty soup is exactly what you need and want for the long winters. Soup is not complicated to make. A combination of a few flavorful ingredients will do the trick. You don't even need a stock or flavor enhancers to make a really satisfying dish. My flavor enhancers are a soffritto (i.e., onions and garlic), good olive oil and cheese.

The recipes in this section prove that simple water and some pantry basics are all you need to make a satisfying soup.

Sure, if you have stock on hand, the soup will benefit from it. But if you don't, there's no reason to not make soup.

ZUPPA
TOSCANA

ACQUACOTTA
COOKED WATER

*A*cquacotta literally translates to "cooked water," which, if you think about it, is really soup. This is an antique Tuscan dish, true *cucina povera*, with many variations. The peasants would use whatever they could forage or find left over from the land owner's harvest, so the dish changed from area to area, season to season.

My version of the recipe uses fresh porcini and spinach as the main ingredients. It doesn't get simpler than this, but the results will blow you away.

4 tbsp (60 mL) extra-virgin olive oil

1 white onion, roughly chopped

1 lb (500 g) fresh porcini mushrooms, cleaned and coarsely chopped

1 bunch spinach, chopped

1 fresh chili pepper, chopped

Salt and freshly ground pepper, QB

3 cups (750 mL) water

1/4 cup (60 mL) freshly grated Parmigiano-Reggiano cheese, for sprinkling

Heat up your olive oil in a deep saucepan, then add onion and cook until soft. Now, add the mushrooms and spinach, and mix together. Add chili pepper, salt and pepper.

Add water, enough to cover the vegetables, and simmer for approximately 15 minutes. To serve, sprinkle with Parmigiano. If you want, you can do what the peasants of old did: put a chunk of stale bread in the bowl first and pour your soup right on top.

Per 4–6 persone

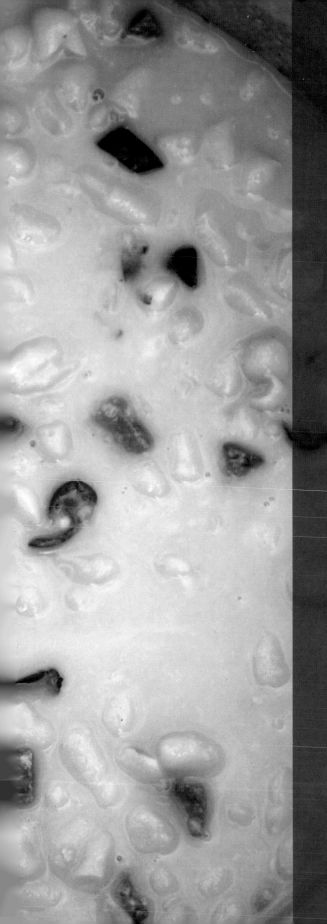

ZUPPA DI FAGIOLI E PANCETTA
BEAN AND PANCETTA SOUP

This bean soup, like the next two, is incredibly fast to make and satisfying to eat, and very economical. All three soups take advantage of canned legumes. There's nothing wrong with using them; just make sure they're not filled with additives, especially sodium. And always give the canned legumes a good rinse before you use them. These soups are true *cucina povera* and really show off the genius of *la cucina toscana*.

- 4 tbsp (60 mL) extra-virgin olive oil
- 2 cloves garlic, crushed
- 3 oz (90 g) pancetta, cubed
- 2 fresh chili peppers, chopped
- 1 can (19 oz/540 mL) cannellini beans, drained and rinsed
- Salt and freshly ground pepper, QB
- 1–2 cups (250–500 mL) water

In a saucepan, heat your olive oil. Sauté the garlic, add the pancetta and cook for 2 minutes, or until the garlic is slightly golden. Now add your chili peppers and cannellini beans and let them cook for a few minutes. Add salt and pepper. I like to take a fork and mash about half of the beans to make a thicker consistency. Of course, if you want a more even consistency, you can use a blender. Either works. Then, add some water, QB, depending on how thick or soupy you want it. Simmer for another 15 minutes.

Per 2–4 persone

ZUPPA DI LENTICCHIE E POMODORI
LENTIL AND TOMATO SOUP

I love lentils. And this soup is another beauty using basic pantry ingredients. For a heartier version that does not betray the soup's *cucina povera* roots, break up some sausage and brown it slightly just before you add the tomatoes.

4 tbsp (60 mL) extra-virgin olive oil

2 cloves garlic, chopped

1 bunch fresh flat-leaf parsley, chopped

2 fresh chili peppers, chopped

1 can (28 oz/796 mL) peeled
plum tomatoes

1 can (19 oz/540 mL) lentils, drained
and rinsed

Salt and freshly ground pepper, QB

Water, QB

In a saucepan, heat up your olive oil. Add the garlic, parsley and chili peppers and sauté for a few minutes, or until the garlic has started to turn golden.

Pour in the plum tomatoes, with the juice, right from the tin. With the back of a wooden spoon, break up the tomatoes into little chunks. You decide the consistency. Then, add the rinsed lentils, salt and pepper. Let this simmer for 15 to 20 minutes, or until the soup has thickened. If you want a "soupier" version, add some water, of course QB.

Per 2–4 persone

ZUPPA DI CECI
CHICKPEA SOUP

This could easily be a side, and if you've ever had a side of chickpeas, rosemary and onions, then you know how fantastic it is. But adding water to it and letting it simmer turns it into a comforting, delicious soup.

4 tbsp (60 mL) extra-virgin olive oil
1 onion, finely chopped
1 sprig fresh rosemary
1 can (19 oz/540 mL) chickpeas, drained
   and rinsed
Salt and freshly ground pepper, QB
2 1/2 cups (625 mL) water
Freshly grated Parmigiano-Reggiano
   cheese, QB (optional)
Extra virgin olive oil, for drizzling, QB

In a saucepan, heat up your olive oil. When it's hot, add the onions and rosemary and sauté until the onions turn slightly golden. Then add the chickpeas and the salt and pepper.

At this point I mash about one-third of the chickpeas with the back of a fork, but you can also wait until the soup is cooked and throw it in a blender. Now add as much water as you want for your soup, bring it to a boil, then lower the heat to medium and simmer for 15 minutes.

Before serving, finish with some freshly grated Parmigiano and a drizzle of olive oil.

Per 2–4 persone

ZUPPA DI ZUCCA E COZZE
BUTTERNUT SQUASH AND MUSSEL SOUP

This is more work than the other soups, but it is well worth the effort. It was inspired by a version of *pasta e fagioli* with mussels that I had in Naples that I loved. The mussels and the squash both have a sweet, delicate taste; they complement each other beautifully.

2 lb (1 kg) fresh mussels	1 onion, chopped
1/2 cup (125 mL) extra virgin olive oil	10 oz (300 g) butternut squash, peeled,
2 cloves garlic, crushed	seeded and cut into cubes
1 fresh chili pepper, chopped	7 oz (200 g) ditalini pasta
1 cup (250 mL) white wine	2–3 cups (500–750 mL) water
Salt and freshly ground pepper, QB	1/2 cup (125 mL) Parmigiano-Reggiano
	cheese

The first thing you have to do is clean the mussels. Put them in a colander and rinse them under cold running water to remove any remaining sand and grit. Mussels often have little threads that look like seaweed hanging off them, called beards. Rip them off. The mussels should be closed. Discard any that are open.

Heat 1/4 cup (60 mL) of the olive oil in a deep saucepan. Add garlic and chili pepper and cook for a minute. Add the mussels, wine, salt and pepper and stir together.

Cover with a lid, allowing the mussels to steam open, which should take about 5 minutes. Cook until all mussels are fully opened. Discard any that are unopened. Let the mixture cool down a bit. Remove and discard the garlic. When the mussels are cool enough to handle, shell them, discarding the shells. Put the mussels back in the broth and set aside.

In another saucepan, heat up the remaining 1/4 cup (60 mL) of olive oil. Add onion, butternut squash, salt and pepper. Cook for a few minutes, until the onion is slightly golden. Then add pasta and mix together. Add most of the water and cook for about 15 minutes, until the pasta is done and the squash is fork-tender. Eyeball it here. If your ingredients need to cook longer and you need more liquid, add more water. To give the soup a creamier consistency, mash 1/2 of the squash with the back of a fork.

Add the mussels and broth to the squash and pasta, and mix. Let it simmer for a few minutes to combine the flavors. Remove from the heat, and add Parmigiano before serving.

Per 4-6 persone

Pasta

Sorry pizza, but pasta is the superstar of Italian cooking. Everyone loves pasta. It's easy to make and satisfying. In spite of this, pasta has no ego: it can be the backdrop to a sauce or the center of attention. If I don't eat pasta at least once a day, I don't feel like I've eaten.

PENNE ALLA TRAPANESE
PENNE TRAPANI STYLE

This dish has a cold, pesto-like sauce, made with a mortar and pestle, that is very typical of the western part of Sicily, in the area of Trapani. This is another example of the simplicity of Italian cooking. Even if I didn't give you exact measurements, I bet you'd still knock it out of the park. Note that some people roast their almonds before making this dish. But if they're fresh, there's no need.

1 lb (500 g) penne

7 oz (200 g) almonds

1 large bunch fresh basil leaves

1 clove garlic

1 lb (500 g) fresh tomatoes, peeled and seeded

Extra-virgin olive oil, QB

Salt and freshly ground pepper, QB

5 oz (150 g) Parmigiano-Reggiano or aged pecorino cheese, grated

If you're using a food processor, you could throw everything for the sauce in at once if you wanted to. But I recommend going old school and preparing one ingredient at a time. It's much more interesting, and you can see the pesto evolve. So, after putting the penne on to cook, start by using a cutting board and a mezzaluna to chop your almonds, basil and garlic into a coarse meal, and then put that into your mortar. Then go for your tomatoes: give them a good rough chop and add them. Now, add a little olive oil, some salt and pepper and, with the pestle, crush and mix everything together into a beautiful pesto. Finish the pesto with your grated cheese of choice and more olive oil if you need it. Taste as you go, so you can adjust the seasonings and find the right texture.

Once your penne is cooked, drain well, reserving a ladleful of cooking water. Put the pasta back in the pot with a little bit of the cooking water and your pesto, then mix to combine the sauce with the pasta, adding more cooking water as needed until you have the desired consistency.

Per 4 persone

PASTA CON POMODORINI
PASTA WITH CHERRY TOMATOES

I made this dish in the breathtaking Amalfi coast town of Positano. We had spent the day at the beach and returned to my friend's house for dinner, expecting that his mom would be home to cook. Instead we found a basketful of cherry tomatoes fresh from her garden—and that was all the inspiration I needed.

This recipe is to be made in midsummer, when cherry tomatoes are sweet, flavorful and readily available. This dish is all about three ingredients: fresh cherry tomatoes, good olive oil and fresh basil.

1 lb (500 g) spaghetti	1 lb (500 g) cherry
5 tbsp (75 mL) extra-	tomatoes
virgin olive oil	Salt, QB
2 cloves garlic	8 fresh basil leaves

You can put this sauce together while your spaghetti is cooking. Start by heating up your olive oil. Crush the garlic cloves with the side of a knife, leaving them whole, and sauté them. This is just to flavor the oil. You're going to remove them once they've done their job. Now, add your cherry tomatoes and a little salt to taste. Sauté the tomatoes until they begin to break down a little, losing their shape and softening. Remove the pan from the heat.

When your spaghetti is al dente, drain it, leaving a little bit of water in the pot. Put the pan of sauce back on medium-high heat. Pour the spaghetti and water into the pan with the tomatoes and mix them together. Sprinkle torn-up fresh basil leaves over the pasta and—*buon appetito!* This dish is so fresh and brilliant that, as much as I like Parmigiano, I don't think you particularly need it here.

CASARECCE CON SALSICCIA
CASARECCE WITH SAUSAGE

This is an easy pasta dish, and a great one to whip up on a weeknight—it'll make you feel like you're enjoying a leisurely lunch at a rustic Italian *agriturismo* in the Chianti hills on a Sunday afternoon. Casarecce is a short dried pasta available in most Italian grocery stores. You can substitute fusilli if you like. For the sausage, I recommend that you use a kind that is already seasoned.

1 lb (500 g) casarecce	1 cup (250 mL) white wine
3 tbsp (45 mL) extra-virgin olive oil	2 cups (500 mL) tomato purée
1 small white onion, finely chopped	Salt and freshly ground pepper, QB
10 oz (300 g) pork sausage, preferably seasoned	1/2 cup (125 mL) freshly grated pecorino cheese

If you want, you can make this sauce while your pasta is cooking. So get the pasta started.

Now heat up a frying pan, pour in the olive oil, add the onion and let it gently mellow in the olive oil. Remove the sausage from its casing and crumble it into the pan. Let that cook until it starts to brown, then add the wine and let that reduce. Now add the tomato purée and season with salt and pepper. Bring the sauce to a light boil, then lower the heat and let it simmer for about 15 minutes.

Meanwhile, drain your casarecce just before it is al dente, reserving about 1 cup (250 mL) of the cooking water in the pot. Put the pasta back into the pot and return the pot to the stove. Add the sauce and mix, and finish cooking the pasta until it is al dente. The sauce will reduce and thicken up and become one with the pasta.

Remove the pot from the heat and throw in the grated pecorino. Mix well and serve. This may be your new favorite pasta.

Per 4 persone

SPAGHETTI ALLA CARBONARA

This is comfort food—like bacon and eggs on pasta. I've always had success with this dish, I think, because it looks so beautiful and it's fun to eat. Not to mention that it has crisp pancetta that everyone loves. It is very quick to make and has to be eaten immediately. I always present it with a raw egg on top so that everyone can stir the yolk in themselves. The hot pasta cooks the egg, but if you're nervous, you can skip the step where you separate the eggs, and add the whole egg to the pot instead. Garnish with some chopped parsley if you like.

1 lb (500 g) spaghetti

2 tbsp (30 mL) extra-virgin olive oil

2 cloves garlic, finely chopped

3 1/2 oz (100 g) pancetta, cubed

4 eggs

1 cup (250 mL) milk

1/2 cup (125 mL) freshly grated
    pecorino cheese

Salt and freshly ground pepper, QB

Start cooking the spaghetti. Timing is important, because you want the pasta to be hot enough to cook the eggs.

Heat up your olive oil in a frying pan over medium heat. Add the garlic and pancetta and fry until the pancetta is golden and beautifully crisp. When it's done, take it off the heat and set aside.

Separate your eggs. If you can, put each yolk in a separate little cup and set that aside until you're ready to serve it. The whites go into a bowl; add the milk, pecorino, salt and lots of pepper, and whisk to combine.

When the pasta is ready, drain it well and put it back into the pot, but not on the heat. Working quickly, throw in the pancetta, with its oil, and the egg white mixture, and stir to make sure everything is coated. The egg whites will cook in the pot and thicken up.

Divide the pasta among 4 serving bowls. On top of each, put an uncooked egg yolk, and serve immediately.

Per 4 persone

SPAGHETTI CON ZUCCHINE DI VILLA MARIA
VILLA MARIA'S SPAGHETTI AND ZUCCHINI

This recipe comes from the Hotel Villa Maria in Ravello, which has a gorgeous garden that supplies the hotel with fresh produce.

Zucchini can sometimes be bland, but the combination of mint and capers really brings it, and the dish, to life.

1 lb (500 g) spaghetti	3 tbsp (45 mL) capers
1 cup (250 mL) extra-virgin olive oil, for frying	1 small bunch fresh mint leaves, finely chopped
4 medium zucchini, sliced	2 tbsp (30 mL) red wine vinegar
Salt, QB	

As in most Italian recipes, you can make the sauce in the time it takes to cook the pasta.

So, while you make the sauce, cook your pasta in a large pot of salted water, as usual, until just slightly before the al dente stage, reserving 1/2 cup (125 mL) of the cooking water.

In a large frying pan, heat up the olive oil and fry the zucchini slices, laying them flat. When they become slightly golden on one side, turn them over. Cook in batches; don't crowd the pan. Put the fried zucchini on a plate lined with a paper towel to absorb the excess oil. Sprinkle salt over the hot zucchini. Turn the heat down to low, and add the capers, half of the mint and the red wine vinegar. Mix that together for about 1 minute. Add half the cooked zucchini, and raise the heat to medium-high. Now add the spaghetti and the pasta water, and finish cooking it by tossing and mixing everything together for another minute. Plate, and then top each serving with the remaining mint and zucchini.

Per 4 persone

MAKING PASTA

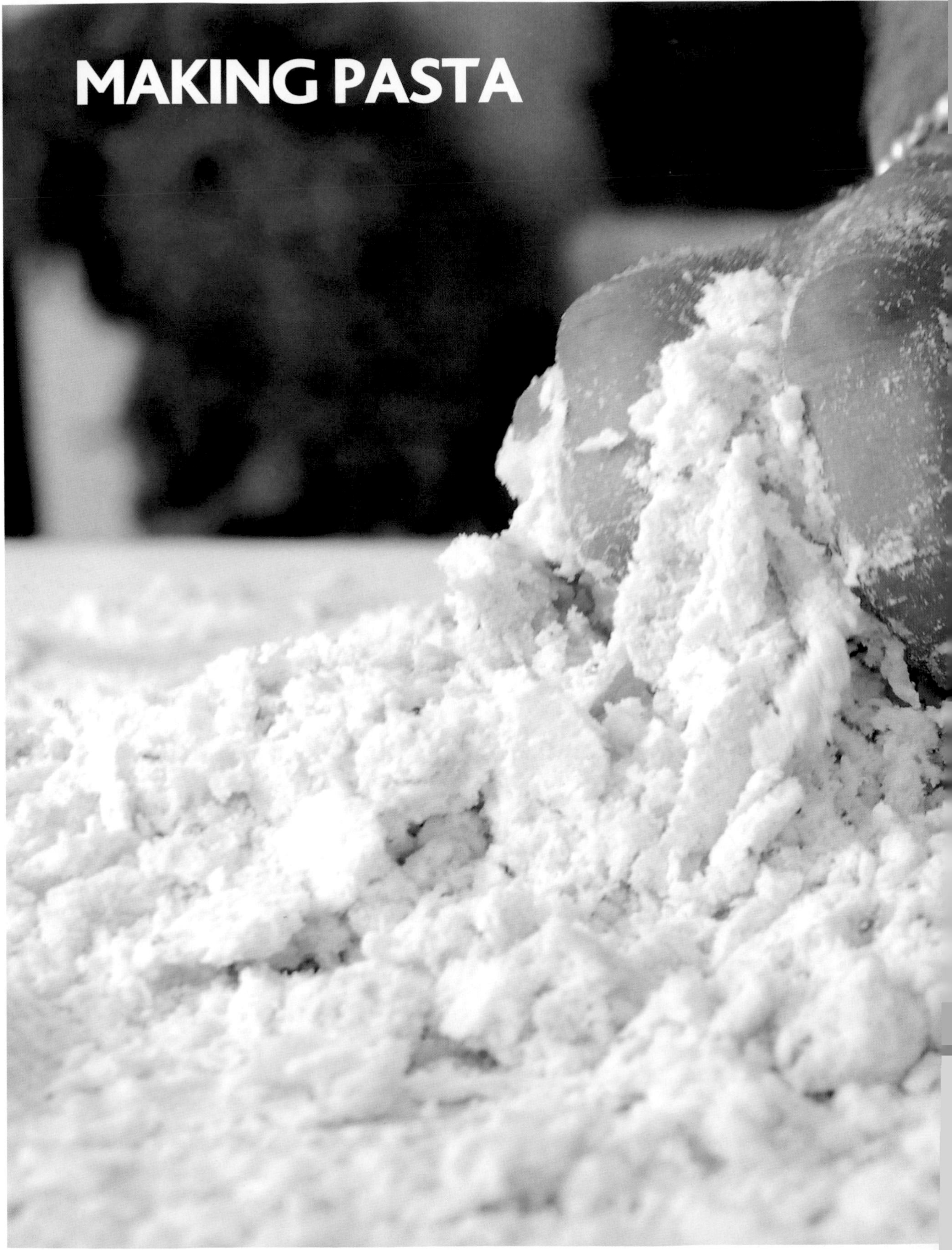

BEPPE'S FAMILY'S PASTA PRANZO

It was supposed to be our last day in Portopalo di Capo Passero in Sicily. But a friend wanted to introduce us to his friend Beppe. And so we all met up at a tiny coffee bar. We hit it off. Within about ten minutes, Beppe was on his cellphone and we were walking down a steep hill towards his mamma's, as the special guests at the Sunday pasta *pranzo*. That's how it happens in Italy. I swear this is how she made her fresh pasta. And let me tell you, it was absolutely delicious—and we spent an absolutely magical afternoon.

9 cups (2.25 L) flour   **Lukewarm water, QB**

So, to make pasta like Beppe's mamma did, here's what you do: Pour the flour on a wooden surface, or in a big bowl. Make a cross in the flour. (There's always divine intervention.) Slowly add lukewarm water, a little at a time, kneading as you go. Knead until you end up with a nice, silky, smooth, elastic dough that holds together in a ball. (Beppe's mom periodically picked it up and slapped it hard on the table.)

Divide the dough into two equal parts; you're going to be making two different shapes of pasta. (This is what Beppe's mom did; it made the final dish very rustic and added some extra texture—which was amazing!)

Lightly flour your work surface and rolling pin. Take half of the dough, tear off egg-sized pieces, and roll them out until you have long strips about 1/8 inch (3 mm) thick. Now set them aside to dry for about 20 minutes. (Beppe's mamma dried hers in the Sicilian sun.)

With the second half of the dough, you're going to make *cavatelli*. So, again tear off pieces and, with your hands, roll them into little logs. Cut these into pieces about 1 inch (2.5 cm) long, and then roll each one against the tines of a fork or along a *ciuliri* to make lines on them. Take the cavatelli and put them aside to dry for about 20 minutes as well. (And if you've got a table where they can rest in the sun, go for it!)

While everything is resting, make some Salsa di Cinque Minuti (page 213).

After 20 minutes, pick up the long, flat pieces from the first batch of dough and cut them into squares of various shapes and sizes. Now you've made *maltagliati*, which translates to "poorly cut pasta."

Now you're ready for the magic. Bring a large pot of water to a boil and salt it liberally. Add both kinds of pasta and cook until they're done, about 10 minutes or until they rise to the surface. Drain. Add the hot pasta to the sauce and mix well. Add grated Parmigiano and mix well again.

Per 6–8 persone

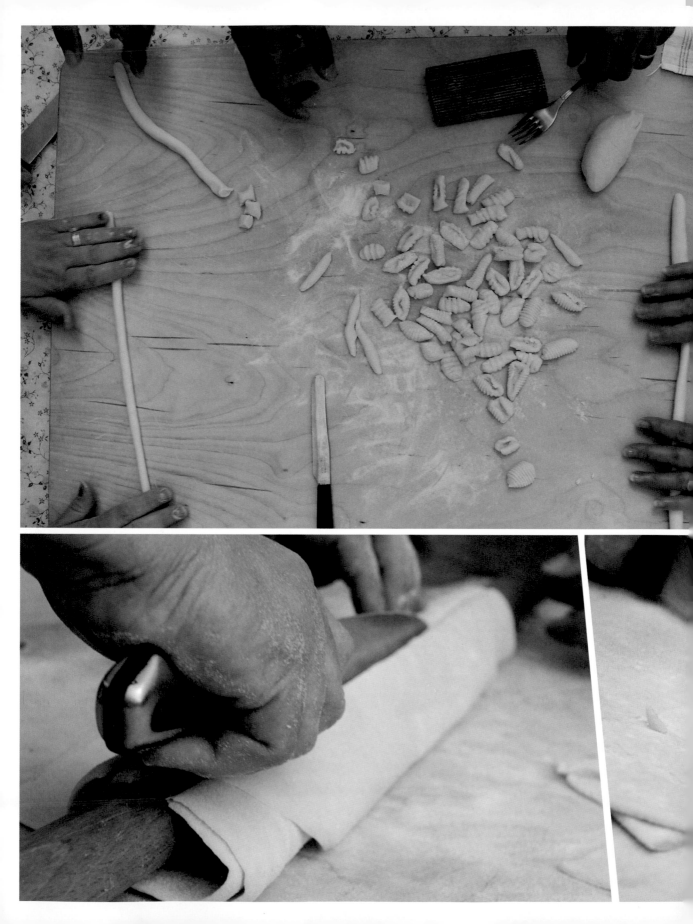

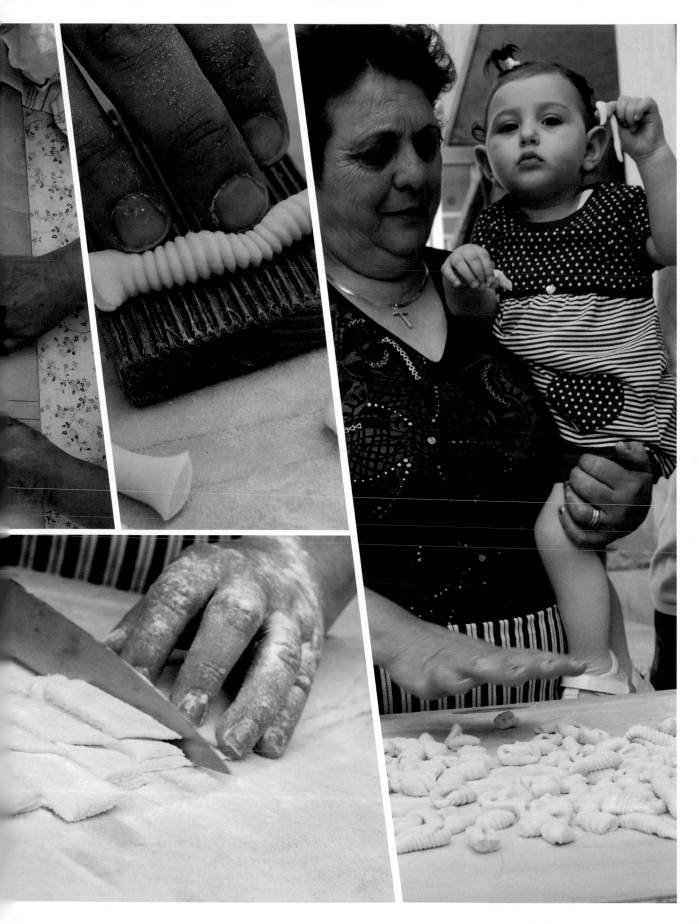

LA POMAROLA DI BEPPE
BEPPE'S TOMATO SAUCE

What a sauce! So delicious and so easy. I like it because you throw everything into the pot at the same time—something I had never seen before.

2 lb (1 kg) cherry tomatoes, halved
2 cloves garlic, chopped
1 red onion, chopped
1/4 cup (60 mL) extra-virgin olive oil
1 bunch fresh basil leaves
Salt, QB

Put everything in a pot on high heat and bring to a boil. Reduce to a simmer and cook until the onions are soft and the sauce develops its flavor, about 30 minutes. Run the whole thing through a food mill, so that it becomes a rich, flavorful puréed tomato sauce.

Makes about 4 cups (1 L)

SALSA DI CINQUE MINUTI
FIVE-MINUTE SAUCE

Use plum tomatoes or purée, depending on whether you prefer a chunky or smooth sauce.

4 tbsp (60 mL) extra-virgin olive oil
1 medium onion, finely chopped
1 clove garlic, finely chopped
Chili pepper flakes, QB
1 can (28 oz/796 mL) peeled plum tomatoes or tomato purée
Salt, QB
5 fresh basil leaves, torn

Heat your olive oil in a saucepan and add the onion, garlic and chili flakes. Gently fry the ingredients together until the onion softens and is slightly browned.

Add the plum tomatoes or purée. If you're using the plum tomatoes, you can either pour them into a bowl and squeeze them with your hands to break them up to a nice texture before you add them to the saucepan or you can put them right into the saucepan and crush them with the back of a spoon to get the texture you like.

Simmer on low to medium heat for 5 to 10 minutes.

Salt to season. Add basil leaves at the very end.

Makes about 4 cups (1 L)

I SCIALATIELLI DI CARLA
CARLA'S NEAPOLITAN PASTA

Carla is a family friend and a terrific cook, especially when it comes to cooking traditional Neapolitan dishes like scialatielli. The name comes from the word *scialare*, which, in the Neapolitan dialect, translates to "enjoy." Scialatielli is a heavy, flavorful dough that makes a denser-than-usual noodle. That's because it uses milk instead of water and adds an egg and cheese to the pasta dough. Scialatielli would classically be made for the Sunday *pranzo* or a special occasion.

4 1/2 cups (1.125 L) flour (tipo 00 or cake flour)	1–1 1/4 cups (250–310 mL) milk
Salt and freshly ground pepper, QB	1 tbsp (15 mL) extra-virgin olive oil
1 large egg	1/2 cup (125 mL) freshly grated pecorino cheese
15 fresh basil leaves, finely chopped	Semolina flour, for dusting

Pour the flour with a little salt and pepper onto your work surface and make a well in the middle. Crack your egg into the well and add the chopped basil, milk and olive oil. With a fork, start to whisk, bringing the flour into the middle, until you have a sticky wet dough. Add the pecorino and knead until you can make a smooth, elastic, soft ball of dough, around 8 minutes. Wrap the dough in plastic wrap. Now both you and the dough can relax for about 1/2 hour.

To make the scialatielli, you can either use a rolling pin or a pasta machine. If you go old school, sprinkle a little semolina flour on your work surface, then rip off a piece of dough and roll it out to about 1/8 inch (3 mm) thick. (Be careful with the amount of flour on the work surface—you don't want to dry out the dough.) Fold it in half and then in half again, then roll it out flat again. Do this two more times.

If you're using a pasta machine, you want it on a fairly thick setting. Put the piece of dough in, and roll it out flat. Take the flat dough, fold it in half, and then in half again, and put it through the machine two more times. Note: When rolling the dough out, don't make it too thin. The beauty of scialatielli is that it's a heavier, thicker pasta. It's not thin like a fettucine! Lay the sheet of pasta on a cutting board and cut it into strips about 1/3 inch (8 mm) wide and about 3 inches (7.5 cm) long.

Before cooking the scialatielli, shake off any excess flour. Now, it will take longer to cook than other fresh pastas because it's thicker, about 5 to 6 minutes.

SCIALATIELLI CON POMODORI E MELANZANE
NEAPOLITAN-STYLE PASTA WITH EGGPLANT AND MOZZARELLA SAUCE

So what do you put on a heavier-than-usual pasta? As it turns out, the traditional Amalfi answer to that question is a heavier-than-usual sauce. This one is made with fior di latte and eggplant. It sounds like it would be too heavy, but as someone who has never said no to seconds of this dish, I can assure you that the pasta and sauce work beautifully together.

1 large eggplant

1/2 cup (125 mL) extra-virgin olive oil, for the eggplant

2 tbsp (30 mL) extra-virgin olive oil, for the sauce

1 onion, chopped

1 can (28 oz/796 mL) peeled plum tomatoes, crushed

Salt and freshly ground pepper, QB

1 batch scialatielli (page 214)

1 large ball fior di latte, cubed

2 tbsp (30 mL) freshly grated pecorino cheese

4 fresh basil leaves, torn

Cut the eggplant into 1/2-inch (1 cm) cubes.

Heat up a frying pan and pour in the 1/2 cup (125 mL) of olive oil. Make sure the oil is hot before you add the eggplant, otherwise it will absorb too much of the oil and become heavy. Add the eggplant and fry until golden. When it's done, remove to a plate lined with paper towel to absorb any excess oil.

In a saucepan, heat up the 2 tbsp (30 mL) of olive oil. Sauté the onions until soft. Add the crushed tomatoes and a little salt and pepper, and let the sauce simmer for 5 minutes.

Now begin to cook your scialatielli by shaking off the excess flour and dropping them into salted boiling water; cook them for about 5 to 6 minutes, or until they rise to the surface. Take them out quickly so they don't overcook. Drain them well and add to the tomato sauce, along with the eggplant, and mix well to combine. Remove from heat. Add the fior di latte, the pecorino and the basil, and stir again to combine.

Serve immediately, and *buon appetito!*

Per 4 persone

STROZZAPRETI
PRIEST STRANGLERS

Lots of pastas have colorful names, but few have as interesting a story as *strozzapreti*: the name translates to "priest stranglers." The legend is that it was invented by frustrated housewives. The local priest would regularly just "happen" to drop in without an invitation at dinnertime and eat at their homes. The women, who worked hard enough during the day, finally got so fed up that they started to make this twisted pasta, secretly hoping that the priest would choke and die! Who knows if it's true? But I can assure you that no one has ever choked on this version. You'll notice that this pasta substitutes tomato juice for the usual water, which gives the strozzapreti so much flavor that they need only a very simple toss with olive oil, fresh rosemary and Parmigiano to complete the dish.

4 1/2 cups (1.125 L) all-purpose flour

3 canned peeled plum tomatoes, finely chopped, with juices

1 egg

Salt, QB

5 tbsp (75 mL) extra-virgin olive oil

1 sprig fresh rosemary, leaves finely chopped

1/2 cup (125 mL) freshly grated Parmigiano-Reggiano cheese

Pour flour onto a work surface. Make a well in the center of the flour and add the tomatoes (with their juices), egg and salt. Combine, and knead until the mixture turns into an even dough. If the mixture is too wet, add some more flour; if it's too dry, add more tomato juice. Knead until you have a round, smooth, slightly elastic ball of dough. Wrap it in plastic, and let it rest at room temperature for about 1/2 hour.

Sprinkle the work surface with a little flour. Take a quarter of the dough and roll it flat. Cut it into strips 1/2 inch (1 cm) wide, then cut each strip into pieces about 2 to 3 (5 to 7.5 cm) inches long.

Using your thumb and index finger, gently pinch each strip in the middle and roll it forwards with your fingers until it gets slightly twisted. Repeat the process until all the dough is used up. Cover up any excess dough with a damp cloth to prevent it from drying out, if you are not using it immediately.

Cook the "priest stranglers" in boiling salted water. When the pasta floats to the surface, after about 2 to 3 minutes, it's done. Drain the strozzapreti, reserving a bit of the pasta water. Put the pasta in a bowl with some of the water. Add the olive oil, rosemary and Parmigiano. Mix well and serve.

Per 6 persone

GNOCCHI DI PORCINI CON BURRO E SALVIA
PORCINI GNOCCHI WITH BUTTER AND SAGE SAUCE

I love gnocchi, and this is one of my favorite ways to prepare it. This recipe takes a simple dish that is essentially potato and flour, and gives it some glamour—and incredible flavor.

For the Gnocchi:
1 cup (250 mL) dried porcini mushrooms
3 large baking potatoes
1/2 cup (125 mL) freshly grated Parmigiano-Reggiano cheese
Salt and freshly ground pepper, QB
2 cups (500 mL) flour, QB

Flour, for dusting

For the Butter and Sage Sauce:
3 tbsp (45 mL) unsalted butter
Fresh sage leaves, QB
1/2 cup (125 mL) freshly grated Parmigiano-Reggiano cheese

For the Gnocchi: Put half of the porcini in a coffee or spice grinder and grind them to the texture of a spice. Chop the rest of the porcini finely.

Boil the potatoes in salted water until tender. Cool, peel and then cut them into quarters. Mash them with the back of a fork, or, for a smoother consistency, put them through a potato ricer. Add the porcini powder and porcini bits, the Parmigiano, salt and pepper, and mix. Now, slowly add the flour. Any Italian grandmother will tell you this phase is all *quanto basta*, using as much flour as you need to absorb the moisture and turn the potato mixture into a dough. So with your hands, mix in the flour, a little at a time, kneading as you go. You know you're done when you can form a ball that is smooth but not sticky, and slightly dry but not falling apart.

On a lightly floured work surface, with the palm of your hand, roll out pieces of dough into logs about 1/2-inch (1 cm) thick. Then cut the logs into about 1-inch (2.5 cm) pieces. Cook the gnocchi in boiling salted water. It will take only 1 or 2 minutes for them to rise to the top, which means they are done. Remove them and reserve a bit of the cooking water.

For the Sauce: Melt butter in a large pan on high heat. Rip up your fresh sage leaves and toss them in. Let that cook for no more than 1 minute. Then add the gnocchi and about 1/2 cup (125 mL) of the cooking water and cook for about another minute, until the sauce becomes thick and creamy. Remove from the heat. Add Parmigiano and fresh sage leaves. Serve immediately.

Per 4 persone

'NDUNDERI CON SALSA AI FUNGHI PORCINI
'NDUNDERI IN PORCINI SAUCE

'Ndunderi is an ancient Italian dish from the Amalfi coast, very similar to gnocchi. I had it for the first time on my first visit to Ravello at the Hotel Villa Maria, at the suggestion of the owner, Vincenzo Palumbo. I loved it!

For the 'Ndunderi:

9 oz (275 g) fresh ricotta cheese

3 egg yolks

A handful of freshly grated Parmigiano-
   Reggiano cheese

Salt and freshly ground pepper, QB

1 1/3 cups (325 mL) flour

For the Sauce:

4 tbsp (60 mL) extra-virgin olive oil

1 clove garlic, chopped

3/4 lb (375 g) fresh porcini mushrooms,
   cleaned and chopped

4 tbsp (60 mL) white wine

10 cherry tomatoes, quartered

4 fresh basil leaves, chopped

2 tbsp (30 g) freshly grated Parmigiano-
   Reggiano cheese

For the 'Ndunderi: It's important that your ricotta is dry. If it's watery, line a colander with cheesecloth, put the ricotta in and rest the whole thing over a bowl. Let it drain overnight in the fridge. If the ricotta is too moist, you'll have to add more flour to the dough, which will make your 'ndunderi too heavy.

Put all the 'ndunderi ingredients in a bowl and get your hands in there and mix it all together until it forms a soft dough. Grab a handful of the dough and, on a floured surface, roll it into a log about 1 inch (2.5 cm) thick. Cut this into pieces about 1 inch (2.5 cm) long. These are your 'ndunderi. Take each piece and, with your thumb, lightly press and roll them down the back of a fork or against a cheese grater to create ridges.

Bring water to a boil, add salt, put in your 'ndunderi and cook until they rise to the surface, about 10 minutes. Drain well and add to your sauce.

For the Sauce: Heat up your olive oil in a frying pan, add the garlic and fry until golden. Add the mushrooms and sauté for a few more minutes. Then add the white wine, tomatoes and basil. Give your sauce a good mix and let it simmer for about 5 minutes. Add the 'ndunderi to the sauce and gently mix to incorporate. Heat it through for no more than 1 minute. Remove from the heat and sprinkle with Parmigiano.

Per 4 persone

PASTA E PATATE
PASTA AND POTATOES

I love pasta. I love potatoes. So if this dish hadn't already existed, I would have invented it. This is a hearty, workman kind of dish. I'll admit it—it's a festival of carbs. But sometimes you need a substantial, stick-to-your-ribs meal of a dish. This is a great opportunity to use up bits of salami or prosciutto or cheese that are slightly past their prime. You can even use your cheese rinds here. Just cut them into chunks and throw them in for that extra cheese surprise. This is also a good time to use up odds and ends of dried pasta you have lying around. The variety will give this dish a really rustic feel.

4 tbsp (60 mL) extra-virgin olive oil, plus extra for drizzling

4 oz (125 g) prosciutto or salami, cubed

1 white onion, finely chopped

1 stalk celery, trimmed and finely chopped

1 carrot, peeled and finely chopped

Salt and freshly ground pepper, QB

1 fresh chili pepper, finely chopped

2 potatoes, peeled and cubed

1 1/4 cups (310 mL) tomato purée

10 oz (300 g) spaghetti, broken into small pieces, or mixed pasta

2 1/2 cups (625 mL) water

1/2 cup (125 mL) freshly grated or cubed pecorino cheese

1/2 cup (125 mL) freshly grated Parmigiano-Reggiano cheese

Heat up your olive oil in a deep pot. Add prosciutto and cook until golden. Then add the soffritto ingredients: onions, celery, carrots, salt and pepper, and chili pepper. Sauté until the onion softens. Add the potatoes and the tomato purée, and stir. Cook for 1 minute. Then add your broken-up spaghetti and mix. Add enough water to cover everything plus 1 inch (2.5 cm) and let it come to a boil. Turn it down to a simmer and let it cook for about 15 minutes, stirring every so often and adding more water if you need to.

When everything is fully cooked, remove it from the heat, add your cheeses and let the dish cool and thicken. I like to eat this at slightly warmer than room temperature.

Per 4–6 persone

PASTA E FAGIOLI
PASTA WITH BEANS

A lot of restaurants in America serve the classic *pasta e fagioli* as a rustic soup. My version is less soup and more of a regular pasta, one that I like eating at room temperature. I prepare this in the late morning and let it rest on my stovetop until lunch. It thickens as it comes to room temperature.

On my last trip to Amalfi, I ate pasta e fagioli at my friends' place where, instead of finishing the pasta with grated cheese, they grated *friselle*, or dried bread, over it. I thought this was absolute genius, and they just chuckled and said that bread was the poor man's Parmigiano (as we sat on the balcony of their multimillion-dollar villa!). The truth is that this wasn't about being frugal. The friselle gave the dish a bit of edge, a really interesting texture and taste.

4 tbsp (60 mL) extra-virgin olive oil

2 cloves garlic, finely chopped

1 small red onion, finely chopped

3 oz (90 g) pancetta, cubed (optional)

2 cups (500 mL) borlotti or kidney
  beans, cooked or canned
  (drained and rinsed)

1 cup (250 mL) tomato purée

Salt and freshly ground pepper, QB

10 oz (300 g) assorted pasta

4 cups (1 L) water (or QB)

1/2 cup (125 mL) freshly grated
  Parmigiano-Reggiano cheese

Grated friselle (or toasted bread
  crumbs), QB

Heat up a pan and add the olive oil. Gently sauté the garlic, onion and pancetta for a few minutes to flavor the olive oil. Add the beans, puréed tomato and some salt and pepper and cook for a few minutes. Add the pasta to the pot and then add just enough water to cover. Give the mixture a good stir to make sure it doesn't stick. Check on it every few minutes, giving it a stir and adding more water if it starts to dry out before the pasta is fully cooked.

The benefit of cooking your pasta in the same pot as the beans is that the starches are released from the pasta, which makes the dish creamy. That, to me, is the sign of a good pasta e fagioli.

Continue to cook on medium heat until the pasta is ready. Now take it off the burner and add your Parmigiano. Mix everything well and let it rest. Don't serve it piping hot; this is a dish that tastes better at room temperature. That allows the flavors to settle in. Before serving, grate the friselle over the dish.

Per 4 persone

SPAGHETTI CON TONNO E CAROTE
SPAGHETTI WITH TUNA AND CARROTS

This recipe is based on a dish that was prepared for me by Angelo, the head chef from the Planeta wine estate. I wasn't sure I was going to like it, because I'm not a big fan of raw carrots. But it was incredible. What won me over was the depth of flavor, especially how the mint infused the whole dish and gave it a gorgeous aroma. And the dreaded raw carrot gave this light, flavorful and fresh sauce just the right amount of texture.

4–6 fresh tomatoes	Salt and freshly ground pepper, QB
2 large carrots, shredded	6 tbsp (90 mL) extra-virgin olive oil
12 fresh mint leaves, chopped	2 lemons
2 cans (each 7 oz/198 g) tuna	1 lb (500 g) spaghetti

Start by making the cold sauce. Dice your tomatoes. Shred your carrots. Chop your mint. Put them in a mixing bowl with your tuna, a little salt and pepper, and a good splash of olive oil and squeeze the lemons over the whole thing. Mix it well and let it rest for 15 minutes to allow the flavors to come together.

You can use any pasta you like, but I think spaghetti works well for this sauce. Cook the pasta until it's al dente, then drain it, reserving a ladleful of the cooking water. Turn off the heat, put the spaghetti back into the pot and add your sauce and water. Mix well and let rest for a minute. This can be served hot or cold.

Per 4 persone

SPAGHETTI ALLE VONGOLE
SPAGHETTI WITH CLAMS

This is one of my wife's favorite dishes, so it's my go-to recipe when I'm in the dog-house. But it's a pleasure to make for her, because she enjoys my version so much more than when she has it at a restaurant. She often feels they're a little too stingy with the clams, and they're too literal with the sauce: the red sauce is too red, the white sauce is too white, with no bits of tomato to give it great flavor. This recipe may seem daunting, but it's actually very easy to make.

2 lb (1 kg) clams (or QB)
4 tbsp (60 mL) extra-virgin olive oil
1 clove garlic, thinly sliced
1 tsp (5 mL) chili pepper flakes (or QB)
1 bunch fresh flat-leaf parsley, chopped

1/2 lb (250 g) cherry tomatoes, quartered
1 cup (250 mL) white wine
Salt, QB
1 lb (500 g) spaghetti

Clean your clams by giving them a good scrub in cold water. Discard any of the ones that are already open.

Clam sauce is dead simple. So, when you're ready to make the sauce, put on a big pot of water for the pasta, let it heat up to a boil and add salt.

In a frying pan on medium heat, heat up your olive oil and add your garlic, chili flakes and parsley. You want these ingredients to gently mellow and flavor the olive oil. When the garlic turns slightly golden, turn up the heat to high, add the clams and the cherry tomatoes, and gently shake the pan. Put the lid on the pan for about 1 minute. Then add the wine and some salt and continue steaming the clams with the lid on until they've fully opened. This should take 3 to 5 minutes. Discard any clams that haven't opened. Lower the heat to medium and, with the lid off, continue to cook your clam sauce so that the wine reduces and the tomatoes break down slightly.

Cook your pasta in the salted boiling water until almost al dente and drain, reserving 1/2 cup (125 mL) of the cooking water.

Pour the pasta right into the pot with the clam sauce and finish cooking it in the sauce. This is important, so that the flavors combine and the starches of the pasta are released and thicken up the sauce. If the sauce is too dry, add reserved pasta water, QB.

Now this is when you break out your best bottle of olive oil. Finish each serving with a drizzle.

Per 4 persone

FORMAGGI

In Italian cooking, cheese, like olive oil, is one of the essential ingredients.

There are fior di latte and mozzarella di bufala from the Campania region, scamorza and ragusano from Sicily, creamy stracchino from Lombardy, burrata from Puglia, or any of hundreds of varieties of cheeses, each with its own personality and taste. Use the real thing, and suddenly your dish has been elevated to a whole new level—and your ingredients are doing all the work for you.

If it says "parmesan," it's not Parmigiano-Reggiano. And there's nothing like the real thing.

SPAGHETTI CAPRESE

When I'm on vacation in Amalfi, I like to go to a place that makes the best fior di latte around. They now know me, because I've been going there for a few years. When I asked why their cheese was so good, they took me over to the stables where they raise and milk their cows. They insisted that I have a taste of the milk just seconds after it came from the cow. How do I describe the taste? It was like a warm, frothy cappuccino. Absolutely delicious.

This is one of my favorite ways to use that incredible fior di latte. It's a spin on the famous Caprese salad and takes only minutes to prepare.

1 lb (500 g) spaghetti
2–3 fresh tomatoes, chopped
8 oz (250 g) fior di latte or
   mozzarella di bufala
Salt, QB

Fresh basil leaves, QB
Fresh oregano, chopped, QB,
   (optional)
Extra-virgin olive oil, QB

Begin cooking your spaghetti. While that's boiling, chop your tomatoes and your fior di latte. Put them in a bowl together. You are going to assemble and season the ingredients as if you were making a Caprese salad. So, add some salt, your basil and, if you want, some fresh oregano. Add your olive oil and mix well. When the pasta is al dente, drain well. Let it sit for a few minutes to slightly cool down; you don't want the hot spaghetti to melt or soften the ingredients. When it's cooled down a little, or is even cold, toss the pasta with the tomatoes and cheese and enjoy. This is one of my favorite summer pastas.

Per 4 persone

SCAMORZA ALLA PIASTRA AL PROFUMO DI LIMONE
LEMON-INFUSED GRILLED SCAMORZA

Scamorza is a fantastic cheese on its own, but when it melts and forms a crust, it's almost indescribably delicious.

You can certainly do this recipe on its own without lemon leaves if you can't find them. You can also grate lemon zest on top of the finished cheese for a slightly infused lemon flavor. If you take the lemon leaf route, make sure you use leaves that have not been treated with pesticides or any kind of spray. Wash them and dry them well.

4 thick slices scamorza cheese
4 lemon leaves or zest of 1 lemon

Use a hot griddle or a non-stick frying pan. Make sure you get the pan very hot. Put in the scamorza slices and let them melt and cook until the cheese starts to form a golden crust. Now, this is where the lemon leaves come in. Flip each piece of cooked cheese onto a lemon leaf so that the uncooked side is on the leaf. Place the leaf in the frying pan and continue cooking until the bottom side melts. The leaf will infuse the cheese with a light lemon flavor. Remove from heat. If you're using lemon zest, top the cheese with it once the second side has melted.

Per 4 persone

SPAGHETTI CON RICOTTA E POMODORINI
SPAGHETTI WITH RICOTTA AND CHERRY TOMATOES

This is a quick, delicious pasta that I especially love making in the summer, when the tomatoes are in season. It's so easy that you can make the sauce while the pasta cooks. There are very few ingredients but, as a friend of mine likes to say about this recipe, "The whole is greater than the sum of its parts would indicate!" I've suggested using spaghetti, but this would also work well with a shell pasta like orecchiette.

1 lb (500 g) spaghetti

4 tbsp (60 mL) extra-virgin olive oil,
   plus extra for drizzling

2 cloves garlic, crushed but left whole

15–20 cherry tomatoes, quartered

Salt, QB

8 oz (250 g) fresh ricotta cheese

10 fresh basil leaves, finely chopped

In a pot of boiling salted water, begin to cook your pasta to slightly before al dente. While the spaghetti is cooking, heat the olive oil in a saucepan, add the garlic, cherry tomatoes and salt, and cook for a few minutes. You want the tomatoes to soften and the garlic to brown just slightly. When that happens, the garlic has done its job, so remove and discard it. Add the ricotta cheese and 1 cup (250 mL) of the hot spaghetti water to the saucepan and begin mixing them into the tomato sauce. The hot water will break down the ricotta and give it a gorgeous, creamy, velvety texture. Now add the drained spaghetti along with 1/2 cup (125 mL) of the cooking water to the saucepan. Toss together and finish cooking for about 30 seconds, so it all combines and the water reduces. Remove from heat, toss in the basil and serve. (If you want, drizzle a little olive oil over each serving.)

Per 4 persone

MARMELLATA DI PEPERONCINO DI GIOIA
GIOIA'S CHILI PEPPER JAM

Italy has some fantastic cheeses. And every one of them deserves to be drizzled with my friend Gioia's incredible chili pepper jam. Its sweet-spicy combination works especially well with sharp cheeses like pecorino. This is really special when you want to snack on some cheese, or as part of a dessert. And believe it or not, this recipe also works with bittersweet dark chocolate.

1/2 lb (250 g) fresh chili peppers, seeded and halved
1 1/2 lb (750 g) yellow and red bell peppers, seeded and halved
2 cups (500 mL) apple cider vinegar
4 3/4 cups (1.175 L) sugar

In a pot, combine all the peppers with the apple cider vinegar. Cover with a lid and cook over medium heat for about 20 minutes, or until the peppers have softened.

Pour the peppers into a colander and drain. With the back of a wooden spoon, press on the peppers to extract any excess liquid, and discard the liquid.

Transfer the peppers to a food mill and purée them. Discard the pepper skins.

Pour the pepper purée into a saucepan and turn the heat to medium-high. Add the sugar a little at a time and mix until it has dissolved.

Lower the heat to medium and continue to cook for about 40 minutes, stirring occasionally. Remove when the mixture reaches a jam-like texture.

Allow to cool and transfer into sterilized jars. Store in the fridge.

Makes 4 x 14 oz (400 mL) jars

Risotto

Outside of Italy, risotto has a reputation of being a difficult or fussy dish. I don't know if that comes from the idea that anything this good has to be complicated to make. Risotto is dead simple and very adaptable. You can make an incredible-tasting one in under twenty-five minutes. And yes, you have to keep an eye on it, but no, you do not have to be chained to your pot, stirring for the entire time.

There are good reasons to add risotto to your kitchen repertoire. It's a beautiful, creamy, comforting dish. And the amazing thing about this is that once you learn the basics, you can create your own recipes, and you can really let your imagination run wild. In fact, when our girls were infants, I would raid our homemade baby-food purées (beets, broccoli, peas, carrots, etc.), which we had frozen in ice-cube trays, and pop a couple of cubes into the risotto. We'd have a delicious, flavorful dish that looked like it took forever and a day to make. This is exciting to me!

And here's another thing that might blow your mind. If I don't have stock on hand, I'll use water. Let's face it: if you don't own a restaurant and you're busy with kids and work and life, you're not making stock all the time. Of course, you can buy some really good vegetable or chicken stocks or broths, but you have to know who is making it, that it's all organic and there are no additives or sodium. And don't use a powdered or sodium-laced cube. So, if you don't have stock, don't sweat it. If you're using great ingredients like good olive oil, good wine and some Parmigiano, that's more than enough.

In Italy, there are three types of rice that are used for risotto: Arborio, Carnaroli and Vialone Nano. Pick the one you like best.

RISOTTO BIANCO
BASIC RISOTTO

Now, here's the technique for a *risotto bianco*, which is a basic risotto.

4 cups (1 L) vegetable stock or water
3 tbsp (45 mL) extra-virgin olive oil
2 shallots or 1 medium white
   onion, minced
2 cups (500 mL) Italian rice
1 cup (250 mL) white wine, at room
   temperature

Salt, QB
2 tbsp (30 mL) butter
1/2 cup (125 g) freshly grated
   Parmigiano-Reggiano cheese
Freshly ground pepper, QB (optional)

Before you start, begin heating up your stock or water to a low simmer.

Step 1: Make a soffritto, or flavor base. Pour olive oil into your frying pan, and on medium heat gently sauté your shallots until they become sweet and soft. Be careful not to brown them.

Step 2: Turn up the heat to medium-high, add the rice and stir so that all the grains of rice are coated in the olive oil. Cook until the rice becomes translucent. Add your wine and let that get fully absorbed by the rice. (If you're using water instead of stock, an extra splash of wine doesn't hurt.) At this point you'll start seeing some of the creaminess coming out of the rice, and the smell will be incredible.

Step 3: Now you're ready to start adding your liquid. So, take a ladleful of the simmering stock or water, and a good pinch of salt, add them to the rice and stir to mix. Let that cook until the rice absorbs the water. Add another ladleful, stir and then wait until that is absorbed. You want to give it a stir every couple of minutes to encourage the starches out of the rice, and also so that nothing is tempted to stick. You will see the dish start to get creamy. Taste as you go along, and if you need more salt, add more! Continue to add the liquid by the ladleful until the rice is al dente—cooked but slightly chewy—and the entire dish is creamy. This will take about 16 to 18 minutes. As for when to stop putting in the liquid? Risotto can be dense and somewhat dry, or somewhat soupy (the perfect consistency is, as the Italians say, *a l'onda*—it should form "a wave" when you move the pot). It's all personal preference.

Step 4: When the rice is cooked, take it off the heat, add the butter, Parmigiano and freshly ground pepper, and mix well. *Basta*, stop, done!

Per 4 persone

RISOTTO BIANCO CON RIDUZIONE DI VINO ROSSO
RISOTTO BIANCO WITH A RED WINE REDUCTION

This is a basic risotto bianco where I change a few of the ingredients and fancy it up to give it wicked flavor. I add some finely diced fennel to my soffritto, some ragusano cheese and a Nero d'Avola wine reduction. If you can't find ragusano, you can substitute a provolone-style cheese.

And if you can't find a Nero d'Avola wine, don't worry—a full-bodied, fruity red wine will do just fine.

Nero d'Avola wine reduction
On high heat, pour 3 cups (750 mL) Nero d'Avola wine into a saucepot, bring to a slight boil and lower the heat to medium. Cook until it reduces and becomes thick like a syrup, and you're left with about 1 cup (250 mL).

4 cups (1 L) vegetable stock or water
3 tbsp (45 mL) extra-virgin olive oil
2 shallots, minced
1 small fennel bulb, minced
2 cups (500 mL) Italian rice
1 cup (250 mL) white wine
Salt, QB
1–2 tbsp (15–30 mL) butter

2/3 cup (150 mL) freshly grated ragusano cheese
1/4 cup (60 mL) freshly grated Parmigiano-Reggiano cheese
Freshly ground pepper, QB
1/2 cup (125 mL) Nero d'Avola wine reduction

Follow the Risotto Bianco recipe (page 251) with these changes:

In Step 1, add finely diced fennel at the same time that you add the shallots. This may take a little longer to cook, so be patient! The flavor the fennel adds is well worth it.

In Step 4, add your ragusano cheese with the butter, Parmigiano and pepper, and mix very well.

To serve, divide the risotto into equal portions, plate, and drizzle the Nero d'Avola wine reduction over top.

Per 4 persone

RISOTTO CON ERBE FRESCHE E YOGURT
RISOTTO WITH FRESH HERBS AND YOGURT

Angelo, the head chef at Planeta winery, has one of the most beautiful herb gardens I've ever seen, just outside his kitchen. One gorgeous June afternoon, he showed me how to make this delicately flavored risotto. There's a lot going on in this garden-inspired dish: each bite gives you a little salty hit from the anchovies against the fresh taste of the lemon and herbs, and the surprising addition of yogurt gives the risotto a silky texture. We enjoyed it—on the patio overlooking the herb beds—along with a crisp Planeta Chardonnay.

4 cups (1 L) vegetable stock or water	1/2 cup (125 mL) plain yogurt
3 tbsp (45 mL) extra-virgin olive oil	Zest of 1 lemon
2 shallots or 1 medium white onion, minced	1 tbsp (15 mL) fresh sage leaves, finely chopped
2 cups (500 mL) Italian rice	1 tbsp (15 mL) fresh mint leaves, finely chopped
1 cup (250 mL) white wine, at room temperature	1 tbsp (15 mL) fresh thyme leaves, finely chopped
Salt, QB	1 1/2 oz (45 g) anchovy fillets, minced
1–2 tbsp (15–30 mL) butter	

Follow the Risotto Bianco recipe (page 251), Steps 1 to 3.

When the rice is done, remove it from the heat and stir in the butter. When it's melted, add the yogurt, lemon zest, finely chopped herbs and anchovies.

Per 4 persone

RISOTTO CON RADICCHIO E FUNGHI
RADICCHIO AND MUSHROOM RISOTTO

This is a beautiful, flavorful dish that contrasts the earthiness of the mushrooms with the slightly bitter taste of the radicchio. I like using a mix of mushrooms for this, but of course you can use your favorite.

6 tbsp (90 mL) extra-virgin olive oil

1 lb (500 g) mixed mushrooms, cleaned and roughly chopped

1 head radicchio, roughly chopped

1 cup (250 mL) red wine

Salt, QB

4 cups (1 L) vegetable stock or water

2 shallots or 1 medium white onion, minced

2 cups (500 mL) Italian rice

1 cup (250 mL) white wine, at room temperature

2 tbsp (30 mL) butter

1/2 cup (125 mL) freshly grated Parmigiano-Reggiano cheese

Pepper, QB (optional)

In a frying pan, heat up half the olive oil until it shimmers. Add the mushrooms and cook until the moisture is released and evaporates, about 5 minutes. When they're done, add the radicchio and cook for a couple of minutes or until it begins to wilt. Add the red wine and some salt, and cook until the wine has evaporated. Set aside.

Follow the Risotto Bianco recipe (page 251), Steps 1 to 3. Just before Step 3 is complete, add the mushrooms and radicchio and mix thoroughly. Let the risotto finish cooking so the flavors can combine.

Remove from the heat and continue with Step 4, adding your butter, Parmigiano and pepper.

Per 4 persone

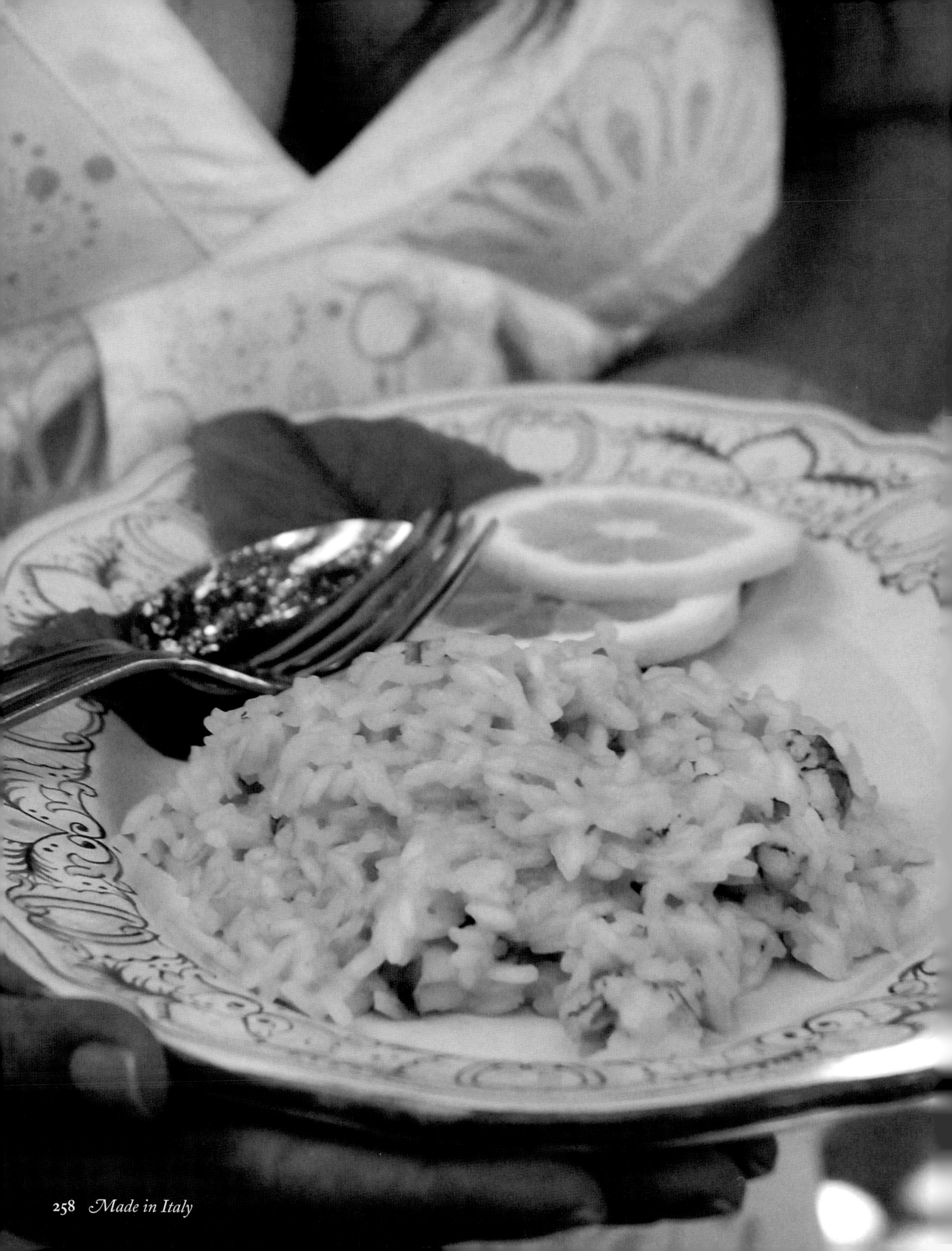

RISOTTO CON GAMBERI E LIMONE
SHRIMP AND LEMON RISOTTO

I had this dish on the Amalfi coast, where they are blessed with fresh, fabulous seafood and where lemons are abundant. This recipe uses the zest and juice of two lemons, so I suggest that you zest them first. Also important: make sure you time the cooking of the shrimp so that they're done just before the risotto is ready—you want the shrimp to stay juicy and firm.

For the Shrimp:

1 lb (500 g) large shrimp, peeled

3 tbsp (45 mL) extra-virgin olive oil

2 cloves garlic, crushed but left whole

Juice of 2 lemons

For the Risotto:

4 cups (1 L) vegetable or fish stock

3 tbsp (45 mL) extra-virgin olive oil

2 shallots or 1 medium white
onion, minced

2 cups (500 mL) Italian rice

1 cup (250 mL) white wine, at room
temperature

Salt, QB

Zest of 2 lemons

2 tbsp (30 mL) butter

1/2 cup (125 mL) freshly grated
Parmigiano-Reggiano cheese

Salt and freshly ground pepper, QB

Chopped fresh flat-leaf parsley, QB
(optional)

Cleaning your shrimp is easy: Peel them, removing the shell and the tail. To remove the dark vein, make a shallow cut down the back with a paring knife, scoop it out and discard. Cut the shrimp into thirds, and set aside.

You want the shrimp to be ready just before the risotto is finished. The shrimp will take 3 to 5 minutes to cook, so have everything ready to go and start the shrimp after your risotto has been cooking for about 11 or 12 minutes.

For the Shrimp: Heat up a frying pan. Add your olive oil and garlic. Fry the garlic for 1 or 2 minutes, until lightly browned. (It's there just to flavor the oil; it'll be removed from the final dish.) Then add the shrimp and the lemon juice and toss the shrimp until they turn pink. Immediately remove the pan from the heat so that the shrimp stop cooking. Remove and discard the garlic.

For the Risotto: In the meantime, follow the Risotto Bianco recipe (page 251), Steps 1 to 3. Just before you add your last ladleful of stock, add the shrimp with the lemon juice and mix. Now, let the shrimp and the risotto finish cooking, so the flavors come together.

Take the rice off the heat, add lemon zest, butter, Parmigiano, pepper and parsley, and mix well.

Per 4 persone

RISOTTO CON CHIANTI, RADICCHIO E GORGONZOLA
RISOTTO WITH CHIANTI, RADICCHIO AND GORGONZOLA

My friend Bernardo's parents are the groundskeepers of a vineyard in Chianti. His mom, Lucia, has made this dish a few times for me during the wine season. I absolutely adore it, which probably isn't surprising, since it uses delicious Chianti as the cooking liquid. This recipe is easy, satisfying and has a no-fuss, rustic elegance to it. I recommend you use a wine that you enjoy drinking, because it is a big part of the flavor of the finished dish. The alcohol burns off and leaves you with a luscious, slightly sweet flavor, which is balanced beautifully by the slight bitterness of the radicchio and the sharp creaminess of the gorgonzola. If you want, you can use half wine and half water or stock. If you can't have wine or prefer not to, you can still enjoy this dish using only stock or water.

4 tbsp (60 mL) extra-virgin olive oil	2 cups (500 mL) Italian rice
2 shallots or 1 medium white onion, minced	5 cups (1.25 L) red wine, preferably Chianti
1 large head radicchio, chopped	3 1/2 oz (100 g) Gorgonzola, cubed
Salt and freshly ground pepper, QB (optional)	1/2 cup (125 mL) freshly grated Parmigiano-Reggiano cheese

In a frying pan over medium heat, heat up your olive oil. When it's hot, add the minced shallots, radicchio and some salt and pepper. Stir and cook until the vegetables are soft. Add the rice and stir. The rice will mix with the vegetables, get coated with the oil and become toasted and translucent. Now is when the magic starts to happen. Add about 1/2 cup (125 mL) of the red wine, stirring so that the rice doesn't stick. When that's absorbed, add more. The risotto will take about 16 to 18 minutes to cook. Remove it from the heat. Stir in the Gorgonzola, and keep stirring until it melts and adds that beautiful, creamy texture and flavor to the dish. Plate, then finish with a good grate of Parmigiano.

Per 4 persone

Secondi

S*econdi* are the main dishes in Italian meals. They consist of *carne*, which is red meat; *pollo* or *pollame*, meaning poultry; and *pesce*, meaning fish. These dishes aren't complicated and seldom are they eaten on their own. They are usually accompanied by some kind of *contorno* (side) or *insalata* (salad).

Carne

IL FAMOSO FILETTO DI MANZO DI ZIA FRANCA
AUNT FRANCA'S FAMOUS BEEF TENDERLOIN

My aunt Franca from Naples is a fabulous cook, and we all wanted her to make this recipe whenever we visited. She made it so effortlessly, with just a few ingredients, yet it has all the attributes that a good beef dish should have. It's also one of my earliest kitchen triumphs—very simple and, believe it or not, very forgiving. Because of the good quality of the meat, I recommend that you serve it medium rare.

6 tbsp (90 mL) extra-virgin olive oil

4 cloves garlic, 2 minced, 2
   crushed but left whole

2 medium carrots, diced

2 stalks celery, diced

1 medium white onion, minced

2 sprigs fresh rosemary

4 fresh sage leaves

2 fresh bay leaves

Salt and freshly ground pepper, QB

Chili pepper flakes, QB (optional)

4 lb (2 kg) beef tenderloin

1–2 cups (250–500 mL) white wine,
   according to taste

For this dish, I suggest using a large pot, one that's significantly larger than the piece of meat, because you want your ingredients to have space. So, in a large pot on medium heat, heat up your olive oil. Add all your vegetables, herbs, salt and pepper and, if you're using them, chili flakes. It's important to cook the vegetables on medium heat because you want to gently coax the sugars and flavors out of them. Let them cook for about 10 minutes, stirring once in a while. When they're soft and starting to color, remove them to a bowl.

Generously salt your beef. Turn up the heat to high and put in the tenderloin, searing on all sides until it browns and forms a crust. Remove the meat. Put the vegetables back in the pot, along with the white wine, and stir everything, scraping up the little bits on the bottom of the pan.

Let the wine boil until it has reduced by half, turn the heat down to medium, put your beef back in and finish cooking for another minute or so on each side.

At this point, turn off the heat and let the meat rest for about 15 minutes. I find this is enough to cook the beef to the medium rare that I like. But if you want it cooked a little more, you can put it into a preheated 350°F (180°C) oven and cook it for another 10 minutes. Or you can slice the meat, put it back in the pan and cook it on medium for another few minutes.

To serve, slice the beef, then plate and spoon the vegetables, herbs and juices over top.

Per 4–6 persone

FILETTO DI MANZO CON RIDUZIONE DI VINO ROSSO
BEEF TENDERLOIN WITH A RED WINE REDUCTION

This is a very simple recipe that looks and sounds much fancier than it is. It's all about a beautiful piece of meat and a flavorful basic wine reduction.

For the meat: ask your butcher to cut it into slices for you, or do it yourself at home before you cook it. The wine reduction should be made in advance so it's ready to go when the meat is done (the meat can be cooked in minutes). For the reduction, use your favorite full-bodied red wine. I like to serve this with Finocchio in Padella (page 94).

For the Red Wine Reduction:
1/2 cup (125 mL) chopped onions
1/2 cup (125 mL) chopped carrots
2 fresh bay leaves
2 fresh sage leaves
1 sprig fresh rosemary
3 cups (750 mL) red wine

1 tbsp (15 mL) unsalted butter

For the Beef:
Salt and freshly ground pepper, QB
4 lb (2 kg) beef tenderloin, sliced to the thickness you like
3 tbsp (45 mL) extra-virgin olive oil

For the Red Wine Reduction: Put all the ingredients, except for the butter, into a saucepan over high heat. Bring to a boil, then turn down to medium-high and continue to cook until the liquid thickens and you're left with about 1 cup (250 mL). Pour through a fine mesh strainer and discard the solids. Put the wine reduction back into the pan over low heat, whisk in the butter and keep warm.

For the Beef: Salt and pepper your meat. In a heavy-bottomed frying pan on high heat, heat up your olive oil until it shimmers, just before it begins to smoke. Then, sear the slices of beef tenderloin for 1 1/2 minutes on each side. This will give you a nice seared outside and, if your slices are about 1 inch (2.5 cm) thick, should take it to medium rare. I'll leave it up to you to look at the slices and decide if you want to let them cook a bit longer to suit your taste. Remove them from the pan. Gently wrap the meat in some tin foil and let it rest for a few minutes.

Pour the wine reduction into the pan in which you just cooked your meat. With a wooden spoon, over medium heat, stir for 1 minute or so to deglaze the pan, picking up those nice bits of meaty flavor that are stuck to the bottom.

Unwrap and plate the meat. Drizzle the wine reduction evenly over all of the pieces.

Per 4–6 persone

BRACIOLE

The beauty of *braciole* is that it ends up being two dishes in one. You cook the meat in tomato sauce. The sauce flavors the braciole, and the braciole does the same favor for the sauce. You end up with a great main dish and a nicely flavored pasta sauce.

4 lb (2 kg) flank steak, cut into 1/2-inch (1 cm) slices

Salt and freshly ground pepper, QB

1 bunch fresh mint leaves, finely chopped

1/2 cup (125 mL) raisins

1/2 cup (125 mL) toasted pine nuts

4 tbsp (60 mL) extra-virgin olive oil

2 cloves garlic, finely chopped

1 medium white onion, minced

Chili pepper flakes, QB

1 cup (250 mL) red wine

4 cups (1 L) tomato purée

Fresh basil leaves (optional)

Your butcher can slice and flatten out your meat for you, or you can do it yourself. In any case, you want the slices to be thin. If you're doing it at home, put the pieces between two slices of plastic wrap and pound until thin.

Lay the slices of meat out, and sprinkle them with salt and pepper.

Place a little bit of the mint, raisins and toasted pine nuts on each piece of the meat, roll the pieces up and use a toothpick to hold each slice together. You can use butcher's twine, but I find toothpicks much easier. And don't worry if any of the rolls unravel in the sauce—you'll just end up with an even more flavorful sauce.

In a large saucepan over medium heat, pour in your olive oil; add garlic, onion and chili flakes, and let them soften and sweeten up the oil. Turn up the heat to high, add your rolled meat and brown on all sides. Add the red wine and let that cook for 1 to 2 minutes to reduce. Add the tomato purée and salt and pepper. Bring to a light boil, then reduce the heat to medium. Let that simmer for 2 to 3 hours, covered.

At this point, you can use the sauce over a pasta as *un primo*, reserving some of it to serve with the braciole as *un secondo*. Add some torn basil leaves, if you want. *E basta!* You're Italiano!

Per 4–6 persone

RAGÙ NAPOLETANO DELLA DOMENICA
SUNDAY'S BRAISED MEATS IN TOMATO SAUCE

This is a Sunday *pranzo* classic for Italian families. And it's another inheritance from *cucina povera*. Here's where inferior tougher cuts of meat are cooked slowly over a long period of time with two fabulous results: first, a sauce (for your pasta) with amazing flavor; and second, a terrific *secondo*—a main course of braised sausages, ribs and chunks of meat in a tomato sauce. It's a thing of beauty. The flavor of this dish is built from the different types of meat that you put in together.

True to the origins of the dish, it's about throwing in whatever meats you have on hand, or that you like. I've listed the meats I like, and of course you can use what you prefer. I don't list amounts, because it's pretty much QB.

(Note: you can get *cotica* from your butcher.)

Onions	Mixed cuts of stewing beef
Extra-virgin olive oil	1/2 lb (250 g) cotica (pig skin)
Sausages, cut up if large	Red wine
Ribs	Tomato purée
Meatballs (page 304)	Salt and freshly ground pepper

Start by dicing onions, then putting them into a hot pan with olive oil and browning them a bit. Add your meat, letting it flavor up in the onion and olive oil and get seared on all sides. Throw in a splash of red wine and, once that's reduced, add enough puréed tomato so that all the meat is entirely covered. Add salt and pepper, bring the sauce to the point where it starts to bubble up, lower the heat to medium and let it cook, covered, for 3 hours.

Remove the meat from the pot. You now have a deliciously flavored meat sauce for your pasta. And the meat becomes the next course—your secondo.

SPEZZATINO DI MANZO CON PATATE
BEEF STEW WITH POTATOES

This is a classic *spezzatino*, a beef stew that is a winter comfort-food classic and that I think is worth having in your repertoire. It's very easy to make, and the long, slow cooking process fills the house with a gorgeous aroma. Don't rush it. If you only have half an hour to make dinner, make this dish another day.

2 lb (1 kg) stewing beef, cut into
   1-inch (2.5 cm) cubes
Salt and freshly ground pepper, QB
1/2 cup (125 mL) extra-virgin olive oil
1 onion, finely chopped
1 carrot, finely chopped
1 stalk celery, finely chopped

1 tbsp (15 mL) tomato paste
1/2 cup (125 mL) tomato purée
3 cups (750 mL) red wine, as needed
2 large potatoes, peeled, cut into
   large pieces
Vegetable stock or water, QB

Generously season your beef cubes with salt and pepper.

Now, make a soffritto, which is the flavor base for your stew and very important. Over medium heat, heat up the olive oil in a pot and add the onion, carrot and celery. Fry them slowly, so that all the flavors and sweetness are coaxed out. When the vegetables soften and are slightly golden, add your beef. Turn up the heat to high and cook until the beef sears on all sides and absorbs the beautiful flavors of the soffritto. Add the tomato paste and the tomato purée and mix. Add the red wine, so that the liquid slightly covers the meat and vegetables. Bring the stew to a gentle boil, then turn down the heat to medium. Let the meat cook for 1/2 hour, uncovered. Then add the potatoes. I like to cut them into big pieces, so they keep their integrity during the long, slow cooking process. Season with salt and pepper. Put on the lid and let the whole thing simmer for at least 1 to 1 1/2 hours, stirring every so often. If you find that it's drying out, you can add vegetable stock or water. You will end up with beef that is fall-apart tender in a thick, sweet sauce. You can eat this as is or serve it over rice.

Per 4 persone

VITELLO CON ERBE FRESCHE
VEAL WITH FRESH HERBS

This is dead simple and literally takes minutes to prepare and to cook. The combination of the chilis, herbs and lemon gives this dish a big flavor payoff for very little effort.

4 tbsp (60 mL) extra-virgin olive oil

2 cloves garlic, thinly sliced

Mixed fresh herbs (flat-leaf parsley, basil, thyme, rosemary), finely chopped, QB

2 fresh chili peppers, thinly sliced

2 lb (1 kg) veal scallopini

Salt and freshly ground pepper, QB

Juice of 1 lemon

On medium heat, heat up your olive oil. Put in the garlic, herbs and fresh chilis. You want to cook this for a few minutes to tease out the sweetness and flavor up the oil without anything burning. Turn up the heat to medium-high. Add the veal, sprinkle with a little salt and pepper and cook on each side for 1 to 1 1/2 minutes. When the meat's done, remove the pan from the heat and squeeze the lemon juice over the scallopini.

Per 4 persone

AGNELLO CON POMODORINI E VINO ROSSO
LAMB IN CHERRY TOMATO AND RED WINE SAUCE

I love lamb. I know not everyone does—maybe because it's sometimes cooked on its own and has an unusual smell. If you're interested in trying lamb, then I think this recipe might be the one for you. It's done with a cherry tomato wine sauce that defeats some of the gaminess and brings out a delectable flavor. Use shoulder or loin chops or a combination.

4 tbsp (60 mL) extra-virgin olive oil	Salt and freshly ground pepper, QB
1 bulb garlic	2 cups (500 mL) red wine
3 lb (1.5 kg) lamb chops	1 lb (500 g) cherry tomatoes, halved
1 sprig fresh rosemary	

Over high heat, heat up your olive oil. Add garlic—usually I cut a whole bulb in half and put it in face down, so that the cut sides are in the oil. Now add the lamb, rosemary sprig and salt and pepper. Sear the lamb on both sides. Add the wine and let that cook until the wine has evaporated. Then throw in the cherry tomatoes, lower the heat to medium and let the whole thing simmer for 1/2 hour.

Per 4 persone

VIVA LA CICCIA

Italy's Dario Cecchini is, arguably, the most famous butcher in the world. For a guy who works behind the counter of a relatively modest butcher shop and oversees a few restaurants in the village of Panzano in the Chianti region of Tuscany, that's really something.

Dario shot to fame when, during the mad cow crisis in 2001, he held a mock funeral in the town square to protest the European Union's ban on selling meat on the bone. That, and his reputation for offering a bit of wine to customers (while quoting Dante with both a twinkle in his eye and the same passion with which he defends his meat), made his store a tourist attraction.

Behind the theatrics is a true artist—a man whose devotion to serving the best to his clients runs deep. Dario is from a long line of butchers, so you could say that butchering is in his DNA. But his commitment to excellence is his own. And it's inspiring. He now has a restaurant above his store that serves some of the best meat I've ever had, including the world-famous Bistecca Fiorentina. (You'll find a recipe for it on page 287.)

BISTECCA FIORENTINA

This is for steak lovers: true Bistecca Fiorentina is a large cut of meat, grilled so that the outside has a beautiful flavor and the inside is rare. There are few ingredients, so it's all about getting the best, grass-fed beef you can find.

1 48-oz (1.5 kg) Porterhouse steak
Salt and freshly ground pepper, QB

Place steak on a very, very, *very* hot grill and cook for approximately 5 minutes per side. Flip it only once and don't move it around. The exact time will depend on how you like your steak, but the true Fiorentina is served with a rare interior. Then stand the meat on the bone and cook for an additional 15 minutes.

Remove steak from grill and season with salt and freshly ground pepper. Serve immediately.

Per 2 persone (but can easily serve 4!)

SUSHI CHIANTI

This is Dario's version of steak tartare. It's his belief that when you use the best meat available (and he has some damned tasty meat), it doesn't need much, except some good Tuscan olive oil. This is a showstopper of a dish, but you want to make sure that you are buying an absolutely fresh bit of preferably organic meat from a butcher you know well. Let your butcher know what you'll be doing with the meat, so you can get proper guidance.

What surprised me was that Dario used two tougher cuts of meat—topside and silverside—and yet, if you follow his recipe, the meat will melt in your mouth.

1 lb (500 g) topside or silverside beef
Salt and freshly ground pepper, QB
Fresh marjoram, QB

Extra-virgin olive oil, QB
Zest and juice of 1 lemon

To begin, check the beef and make sure to cut out any sinews. Finely chop the meat and give it a good hammering with a meat tenderizer until it has the texture of hamburger. Now, do as Dario does and add some salt, pepper and marjoram, and pound the meat again. This, Dario says, punches the flavor right into the beef. Then finely chop it again and transfer it to a plate. Finish it with the best olive oil you have and squeeze the juice of a fresh lemon right over it. Add the zest of the lemon and serve immediately. Dario serves his Sushi Chianti with chopsticks.

Per 2–4 persone

CONIGLIO CON ROSMARINO DI EMMA-BUNNY
EMMA-BUNNY'S RABBIT WITH ROSEMARY

Ilove rabbit. It's a healthy, lean, succulent white meat. In fact, our daughters' first meat was rabbit, precisely because it's an animal that, for the most part, eats only greens, so you know the meat is free of additives and healthy. (Ironically, my daughter Emma, whose nickname from birth has been Emma-Bunny, loves eating rabbit!)

The taste is not unlike chicken, but sweeter and more flavorful. For this recipe, I would recommend that you ask your butcher to prepare the rabbit so that it's cleaned and cut, and ready to go for you.

Now, I know people who are happy to eat chicken or beef but who cringe at the thought of eating rabbit, which is, of course, cuter than those other animals. If you are like them, don't worry—this recipe will also work with chicken.

3 1/2 lb (1.6 kg) rabbit, cleaned and cut into pieces	1 onion, chopped
Salt and freshly ground pepper, QB	3 cloves garlic, crushed, but left whole
All-purpose flour, for dredging	6 fresh sage leaves
4 tbsp (60 mL) extra-virgin olive oil	2 sprigs fresh rosemary
	2 cups (500 mL) white wine
	2 tbsp (30 mL) unsalted butter

Generously season the rabbit pieces with salt and pepper. Dredge in flour and shake to remove the excess. In a large frying pan over medium heat, heat up the olive oil and add the onions, garlic and your herbs. Let that cook until the onions soften and the ingredients flavor up the olive oil. Turn up the heat to medium-high and add your rabbit pieces. Brown on all sides. Pour in the wine and when it comes to a light boil, reduce the heat to medium low. Put in the butter and season lightly with salt and pepper. Now it's just about letting the rabbit cook and the white wine sauce thicken. This will take about 30 minutes. Turn the pieces over every so often so that they cook evenly.

I like to put the pieces of rabbit on Giorgie-Porgie's Polenta (page 292) and spoon the white wine sauce over it.

Per 4 persone

GIORGIE-PORGIE'S POLENTA

My daughter Giorgia loves this so much that I've started calling her Giorgie-Porgie. She always asks for *polenta con sugo* for dinner. It's not so surprising: polenta has a texture a bit like porridge and is a perfect foil for whatever you put on it.

Polenta can be served as a starch, like bread, or as a mashed potato or pasta substitute. It can also be grilled or fried like french fries, or even served cold. All of this from a humble, porridgy dish of corn grits and water! There are many variations in the grind of the polenta, but I recommend finely ground, quick-cooking cornmeal from Italy.

4 cups (1 L) water
A good pinch of salt
1 cup (250 mL) finely ground, quick-
   cooking polenta

Freshly grated Parmigiano-Reggiano
   cheese, QB
Extra-virgin olive oil, QB

Pour the water and the salt into a pot. Over medium-high heat, heat until the water is just under a boil. Then start adding your polenta, a little at a time, letting it fall through your hand, a bit like sand at the beach. Whisk the mixture continually as you do this. Once all the polenta has been added, lower the heat to medium and continue stirring until the mixture thickens up. It's important to stir so there are no lumps.

You'll know your polenta is ready when it's creamy and all the water has been absorbed. When that happens, take it off the heat.

You can serve it as is, with some freshly grated Parmigiano and a drizzle of olive oil.

Per 2–4 persone

Cinghiale, or wild boar, is a Tuscan specialty. This is not farmed meat; cinghiali roam the hills of Tuscany. During the fall there's a government regulated cull and then hundreds of Tuscan chefs go into action making everything from wild boar salami to sauces and fabulous stews. Like most grass-fed, free-range meat, it is leaner than farmed and really flavorful. If you can't find wild boar, you can still make wonderful Tuscan-style dishes with other game, like bison or elk.

SPEZZATINO DI CINGHIALE
WILD BOAR STEW

Cinghiale dishes are popular in Tuscany in the fall, and this recipe is a classic. If you can't find it, you can substitute another wild game meat like bison, elk or moose—or just use beef.

4 tbsp (60 mL) extra-virgin olive oil
1 carrot, roughly chopped
1 stalk celery, roughly chopped
1 onion, roughly chopped
2 lb (1 kg) wild boar, cubed
Salt and freshly ground pepper, QB

1/2 tsp (2 mL) nutmeg
1 cup (250 mL) red wine
1 can (28 oz/796 mL) peeled plum
   tomatoes, puréed
1 cup (250 mL) beef stock

Start with your soffritto. Over medium-high heat, heat up your olive oil in a large stewing pot and add carrots, celery and onion. Cook until vegetables soften. Add the wild boar and season with salt, pepper and nutmeg. Mix together for a few minutes to combine the flavors, then add the wine. Allow the wine to reduce until syrupy. Add tomato purée, beef stock and more salt to taste. Cover with a lid and cook for 2 hours, until you're left with a thick sauce and the meat is soft and tender.

Per 4 persone

SUGO DI CINGHIALE
WILD BOAR SAUCE

This is a hearty Bolognese-style sauce using wild boar. Over pasta or polenta, it is to die for.

4 tbsp (60 mL) extra-virgin olive oil

1 carrot, finely chopped

1 stalk celery, finely chopped

1 onion, finely chopped

1 lb (500 g) wild boar, minced

Salt and freshly ground pepper, QB

1/2 tsp (2 mL) nutmeg

2 cups (500 mL) red wine

3 tbsp (45 mL) tomato paste

Over medium heat, heat up your olive oil in a saucepan and sauté the carrots, celery and onion until they're soft. Add the minced wild boar, mix with the vegetables and continue cooking until the meat is browned. Add salt, pepper, nutmeg and half of the wine. Allow the wine to reduce until syrupy. Then add the tomato paste, mix well with the meat and add the remaining wine. Let the sauce simmer on medium heat for about 20 minutes.

Per 4 persone

SALSICCE AL FORNO CON PEPERONI, PATATE E CIPOLLE
ROASTED SAUSAGES, PEPPERS, POTATOES AND ONIONS

This is classic Southern Italian cooking. It's no-nonsense, nothing complicated, just good, hearty, honest and delicious. It's *quanto basto*, and dead simple.

In fact, if you're busy and don't have time, but want something hearty, then this is the recipe for you. Once you've prepared your vegetables, your oven does all the work. You can use any of your favorite roasting vegetables. The traditional version is with potatoes, peppers and onions. I sometimes use sweet potatoes, fennel and carrots.

1 lb (500 g) potatoes, peeled and cut into wedges

2 large red or white onions, peeled and cut into wedges

2 large red peppers, cored, seeded and cut into large pieces

Salt and freshly ground pepper, QB

Extra-virgin olive oil, QB

1–2 lb (500 g–1 kg) pork sausages

Preheat your oven to 450°F (230°C).

Put all your vegetables into a shallow large roasting pan and season with salt, pepper and olive oil. I find that when roasting potatoes, you always need more salt than you think. With your hands, get in there and mix well; you want to make sure all the vegetables are fully coated and seasoned. Throw it all into a hot oven and let it roast for about 40 minutes, stirring a few times so everything gets cooked well and becomes crisp. That's my favorite part of this dish—the crispy bits of potatoes and onions.

Pierce the sausages in 3 or 4 places and add to the pan. Cook for another 20 minutes, or until the sausages are fully cooked and golden. You can turn them every so often if you want to brown them on all sides.

Per 4 persone

EVERYONE LOVES POLPETTE

What is it about the meatball that makes it one of life's little pleasures? It is, after all, about as humble as it gets, and yet it's also universally recognized as a comfort food. So, in this section I've also included a few non-meat "meatball" options for the vegetarians out there who crave that flavor and texture.

Whether they're meat or fish or vegetarian, meatballs, or *polpette* as Italians call them, live and die based on what I call flavor enhancers and accessories, that is, the ingredients you use to hold them together and the sauces that you cook them in. Here are some of my favorites.

LE MIE POLPETTE PREFERITE
MY ALL-TIME FAVORITE MEATBALLS

These meatballs are outstanding because of the crust that you get when you fry them and the gorgeous wine sauce that comes from deglazing the pan. They're absolutely delicious—moist and full of flavor, with a silky texture. Some meatball recipes can be dry and heavy (I secretly love that kind too), but here the ricotta's job is to help bind the meat together and keep it moist. And let me tell you, my friends, it does its job well. The sun-dried tomatoes add an explosion of sweetness.

For the Meatballs:

1 lb (500 g) extra-lean ground beef

3 1/2 oz (100 g) fresh ricotta cheese

1 egg

10 sun-dried tomatoes, finely chopped

1 cup (250 mL) freshly grated
   Parmigiano-Reggiano cheese

Salt and freshly ground pepper, QB

Flour, for dredging

For the Wine Sauce:

4 tbsp (60 mL) extra-virgin olive oil

2 cloves garlic, crushed whole

5 sun-dried tomatoes, halved

1 cup (250 mL) white wine

For the Meatballs: Put ground beef, ricotta, egg, sun-dried tomatoes, Parmigiano and salt and pepper into a mixing bowl. Get your hands in the bowl and mix well until the ingredients are evenly incorporated.

Roll bits of the mixture into the size and shape of golf balls and then give them a gentle pat to slightly flatten them, so they can cook evenly. Now, to help with that beautiful crust, lightly dredge them in flour, shaking off any excess.

For the Wine Sauce: In a large frying pan, on high heat, heat up the olive oil, and when it's very hot, add the meatballs, garlic and halved sun-dried tomatoes.

Fry meatballs until golden on both sides, but be careful that you're not burning your garlic or sun-dried tomatoes. If they start to burn, remove them. Add the wine, and if you have taken out the garlic and sun-dried tomatoes, put them back in. When the wine reaches a slight boil, lower the heat to medium and let the whole thing cook for 5 minutes, or until the wine is reduced by two-thirds and forms a nice, thick, sweet sauce.

If you want your polpette in tomato sauce, you can prepare them in one of two ways: dredged in flour, fried and then finished in a simple tomato sauce for 5 minutes; or slow cooked in sauce for 45 minutes—just don't dredge them in flour.

Per 4–6 persone

POLPETTE IN SUGO DI POMODORO
MEATBALLS IN TOMATO SAUCE

Meatballs in tomato sauce is one of the great clichés of Italian cuisine. Who cares? I can live with that, especially when they're this good. You can make these beauties two ways. Both are in tomato sauce; one way is cooked in tomato sauce, the other way is just fried and finished in tomato sauce. Either way, they're a delicious thing, and the best part is that there's a lot of *quanto basta* in these recipes. After all, every Italian son thinks his mother's meatballs are the best.

For the Meatballs:
2–3 slices white bread, crusts removed
1 cup (250 mL) milk
1 lb (500 g) ground beef
1 lb (500 g) ground pork
2 eggs
1 cup (250 mL) freshly grated
   Parmigiano-Reggiano cheese
1 bunch fresh flat-leaf parsley, chopped

Salt and freshly ground pepper, QB

For the Sugo:
4 tbsp (60 mL) extra-virgin olive oil
1 small onion, finely chopped
1 cup (250 mL) red wine
4 cups (1 L) tomato purée
Salt and freshly ground pepper, QB

I make my meatballs in a big bowl because everything goes in together and I like to have room to get my hands in there and really mix things up.

Soak your bread in milk for a few minutes so the bread softens up. While it's soaking, put the meat in the bowl along with what I call my binders and flavorings—

the eggs, Parmigiano, half of the parsley and the salt and pepper. Squeeze the bread to get rid of the excess milk, and then crumble it right into the big bowl. This is going to make your meatballs soft and moist.

Now get your hands in there and mix the whole thing together until you can form little meatballs that hold together. That's why I say it's all *quanto basta*—because you can eyeball it all and not worry about being so precise. If you want to add a little more or less of an ingredient, go for it. After all, Italian *mamme* all over the world have been adapting recipes to their own way since the beginning of time.

From here on, you have two options:

Option one gives you a meatball with a slightly seared exterior. In a saucepan, heat the olive oil over medium-high heat. Add the meatballs and slightly brown them on all sides. Add the remaining parsley and the onions, and cook until the onions start to soften. Pour in the red wine and let the mixture cook for 1 to 2 minutes, or until the wine reduces by half. Then add the tomato purée, salt and pepper. Let the sauce come to a slight boil and then turn it down and let it simmer for 30 minutes.

Option two gives you a more tender meatball. Heat up your saucepan on medium. Add the olive oil, onions and the remaining parsley, and cook until the onions have softened. Add the red wine and let the mixture cook for a few minutes. Then add the tomato purée, salt, and pepper and bring that to a boil. Now in go your meatballs. Turn the heat down to a simmer and let the dish cook for 45 minutes.

You can't go wrong either way. Now make some spaghetti and go cliché!

Per 6–8 persone

POLPETTE DI TONNO
TUNA BALLS

This is not a classic Italian recipe, but I've taken the old-school method of flavoring and given it a modern twist. Use the freshest sushi-grade tuna you can find. And then, of course, it's all about great taste.

For the Tuna Balls:

1 lb (500 g) sushi-grade tuna, minced

1/2 cup (125 mL) bread crumbs

1/2 cup (125 mL) raisins

1/2 cup (125 mL) pine nuts

1 cup (250 mL) freshly grated Parmi-
    giano-Reggiano cheese

1/2 cup (125 mL) white wine

1/4 cup (60 mL) flour (optional)

1/2 cup (125 mL) sesame seeds

4 tbsp (60 mL) extra-virgin olive oil

For the Balsamic Sauce:

2 cups (500 mL) balsamic vinegar

1 sprig fresh rosemary, stem discarded,
    leaves chopped

In a mixing bowl, combine tuna, bread crumbs, raisins, pine nuts, Parmigiano and wine and mix together well. As always, I like to use my hands, because you can get things well combined. When it's mixed, see if you can roll the tuna into little balls that don't fall apart. (If you can't, then add flour to the mixture, a little at a time, until the balls hold together. Go easy—you don't want to weigh them down.)

Now, wet your hands and make tight, compact little balls. Spread the sesame seeds onto a plate and roll the balls in the seeds to coat.

Because of the delicate meat, it's important to use a non-stick frying pan. Over medium heat, heat up your olive oil until it's smoking. Then, gently place the tuna balls in the oil and fry on all sides until golden brown. Because you're using sushi-grade tuna, don't worry about undercooking it. You actually want the meat to be raw in the middle.

To make the balsamic sauce, heat up balsamic vinegar and rosemary in a saucepan. When the vinegar comes to a boil, lower the heat to medium and cook until it reduces by two-thirds and you're left with a beautiful, thick, sweet syrup.

Drizzle balsamic sauce over the meatballs.

Per 6 persone

POLPETTE DI MELANZANE
EGGPLANT BALLS

These are meatless. But don't be fooled—they're just as tasty and satisfying as any meatball in this chapter.

2 medium eggplants, cubed

2 slices stale bread, crust removed

1 cup (250 mL) milk

2 eggs

1 cup (250 mL) freshly grated
   pecorino cheese

1 cup (250 mL) freshly grated
   Parmigiano-Reggiano cheese

Salt, QB

1/2 cup (125 mL) bread crumbs (or QB)

1/2 cup (125 mL) flour (or QB)

Cook the eggplant in boiling salted water for 5 minutes. Drain well and let cool. Squeeze out as much water as you can.

While the eggplant is cooling, combine the bread and milk, and let sit for a few minutes. Remove the bread and squeeze out the excess liquid.

Into a large bowl, put the eggplant and crumble the bread. Add the eggs, cheeses and salt and mix together with your hands. For the bread crumbs and the flour, it's all *quanto basta*. Their main purpose is to help bind the balls and to absorb any excess moisture. So, use your judgment and add a little of the bread crumbs and flour at a time, until you get a nice consistency that you can roll into a compact ball.

To cook them, make my Salsa di Cinque Minuti (page 213), bring it to a light boil, add the eggplant balls and turn the heat down to medium. Let them cook at a simmer for about 15 minutes.

When they're done, plate and top each serving with Parmigiano.

Per 4–6 persone

POLPETTE DI ZUCCHINE
ZUCCHINI BALLS

These are wicked. The combination of zucchini and mint, blended with beautiful cheeses and then fried to a golden crust, is absolutely delicious!

For the Tomato Salad:
20 cherry tomatoes, halved
14 fresh basil leaves, torn
3 tbsp (45 mL) extra-virgin olive oil
Salt and freshly ground pepper QB

For the Zucchini Balls:
3 large zucchini, chopped
1 cup (250 mL) cubed smoked scamorza cheese

1 cup (250 mL) cubed pecorino cheese
1 small bunch fresh mint leaves, finely chopped
2 eggs
1 cup (250 mL) bread crumbs, plus extra for coating
Salt and freshly ground pepper QB
Flour for dredging
1 cup (250 mL) extra-virgin olive oil

Start by making the tomato salad. Toss the halved cherry tomatoes, basil, olive oil and salt and pepper together in a bowl. Set aside.

Boil the zucchini in salted water for 5 minutes. Drain, and when the zucchini is cool enough to handle, squeeze out the excess water.

In a mixing bowl, combine zucchini, the cheeses, mint, eggs, bread crumbs and salt and pepper. Mix well until ingredients are well combined. Roll the mixture into the shape and size of golf balls and then gently flatten with the palm of your hand. Lightly dredge them in flour. Heat your olive oil in a frying pan, and when it's hot, put in the balls and fry until they're golden and crispy on both sides. Remove them to a plate covered with an absorbent paper towel to soak up any excess oil.

Serve the zucchini balls with a little of the tomato salad on top.

Per 4–6 persone

Pollo

POLLO AL LIMONE
CHICKEN WITH LEMON

This is a great dish to make, especially if you find yourself with some fresh, juicy lemons. Don't let the simplicity fool you—every ingredient carries more than its weight.

2 lb (1 kg) boneless, skinless chicken breasts, or scallopini

Salt and freshly ground pepper, QB

Flour, for dredging

3 tbsp (45 mL) extra-virgin olive oil

2 garlic cloves, whole

2 tbsp (30 g) capers

1/2 cup (125 mL) white wine

1–2 tbsp (15–30 mL) unsalted butter

Zest and juice of 1 lemon

Chopped fresh flat-leaf parsley, QB

If you're not using scallopini, pound your chicken breasts until they're about a 1/4 inch (5 mm) thick. Season with salt and pepper on both sides and dredge in flour.

On medium-high heat, heat up your olive oil in a frying pan, and when it's hot, add the garlic and capers and cook for 1 minute or so. Add your chicken breasts to the pan and lightly brown them on both sides. Pour in the wine, add the butter, lemon zest and juice, then some salt and parsley. Let that cook for a couple of minutes, until the wine reduces and the sauce thickens up.

Per 4 persone

POLLO ALLA CACCIATORA
CHICKEN CACCIATORE

This is my favorite chicken dish, probably because it slow cooks in a combination of the wine and the fresh cherry tomatoes, which gives it a really sweet taste.

I like using cherry tomatoes, but you can certainly use canned crushed tomatoes. In either case, you want to just have little bits of tomatoes and not a runny sauce.

Extra-virgin olive oil, QB

3 1/2 lb (1.6 kg) chicken, cut into
   pieces, skin on

Salt, QB

Chili pepper flakes, QB

2 cloves garlic, finely chopped

1 onion, finely chopped

1 sprig fresh rosemary

1 cup (250 mL) white wine

1 bunch fresh flat-leaf parsley,
   finely chopped

2 1/2 cups (625 mL) cherry
   tomatoes, halved

Water or chicken stock, QB (optional)

In a large frying pan over high heat, heat up the olive oil.

Put the chicken pieces in, skin side down, and brown them. Then turn them over and brown the other side. Remove the chicken and sprinkle with salt. Add the chili flakes, garlic, onions and rosemary sprig to the frying pan and cook until the onions start to turn golden. Put your chicken back in, throw in your white wine, parsley and the cherry tomatoes and reduce the heat to medium. Bring to a simmer. Add a little bit more salt. Put the lid on and let the whole thing cook for another 30 minutes, turning the chicken pieces every so often. If the sauce is drying out too fast, you can add a splash more wine (or water or chicken stock). You don't want a watery sauce, though, so add only a bit at a time.

Per 4 persone

SALTIMBOCCA DI POLLO
CHICKEN THAT "JUMPS" IN YOUR MOUTH

This is a twist on the classic Roman dish *veal saltimbocca*. Instead of veal, I'm using chicken for the same *favoloso* result. Some recipes call for adding a little chicken stock to help cook your meat. This, to me, is something that works if you're cooking in a restaurant kitchen. But at home, I want things delicious and simple, and I'm not one of those people who has a stash of homemade chicken stock on hand. So this version uses sweet Marsala wine instead. My favorite thing about this dish is the crispy sage against the salty prosciutto—which justifies its name!

Flour, for dredging

Salt and freshly ground pepper, QB

4 8-oz (250 g) chicken breasts

8 thin slices prosciutto

8 large fresh sage leaves, plus extra
   for sauce

4 tbsp (60 mL) extra-virgin olive oil

1 1/4 cup (310 mL) Marsala wine

1 bunch fresh flat-leaf parsley, chopped

2 tbsp (30 mL) butter

Pour some flour onto a plate and season with salt and pepper.

With a meat tenderizer, pound the breasts until they're about 1/4 inch (5 mm) thick, then cut them in half so you have 8 pieces. Season the chicken with salt and pepper, and lay 1 slice of prosciutto and 1 sage leaf on each piece. Secure the sage and prosciutto to the chicken by threading a toothpick through the layers. Dredge each piece in the seasoned flour to coat both sides, and shake off the excess.

Now the fun part. In a large sauté pan over high heat, heat the oil until it starts to smoke. Add the chicken and some extra sage leaves. Sauté until the chicken is golden on both sides and the sage leaves are crisp. Add the Marsala and continue cooking over high heat until the wine reduces by half. Remove the chicken and the crisped sage leaves to a plate. Add the parsley to the frying pan, whisk in the butter and cook for a minute. To serve, plate the chicken, add a few crispy sage leaves to each dish and finish with the sauce.

Per 4 persone

POLLO CON ROSMARINO E PEPERONCINO
CHICKEN WITH CRISPY ROSEMARY AND CHILI

This may be the easiest, fastest, most delicious chicken dish in the world. It takes minutes. You can make as few or as many chicken breasts as you want, to your taste.

This recipe requires flattened chicken, so either buy scallopini or get boneless, skinless chicken breasts and pound them to a 1/4 inch (5 mm) thickness.

Sprinkle a little salt and pepper over both sides of the chicken breasts. Heat a pan. Add olive oil. When it gets hot, put in the chicken breasts and a couple of whole garlic cloves. Cook until the chicken is brown on one side, and add a chopped chili pepper and rosemary leaves. Flip the chicken over and cook until the second side is golden and the meat is cooked through. Just before the chicken is ready, add 1/2 cup (125 mL) of white wine and let that reduce until syrupy.

INSALATA DI POLLO E RADICCHIO
CHICKEN AND RADICCHIO SALAD

This gorgeous salad can—and I think *should*—be made well in advance of serving. It's a perfect dish for a party or picnic. When the salad sits for a bit, the seasonings can really work their magic. Since radicchio is hearty, it won't wilt or get soggy.

You can use the Pollo con Rosmarino e Peperoncino for this salad (see above), or any cooked chicken. Slice it into strips and put it into a bowl with torn radicchio. Slice some red chilis and add them to the bowl. Season with olive oil, balsamic vinegar and salt, all QB.

I recommend preparing this at least 1 hour before serving, so all the flavors have time to combine.

Pesce

DENTICE AL FORNO
BAKED DENTEX

Dentice (known in English by the rather unfortunate name "dentex") is not a dental product, but rather a fish common to the Mediterranean. And a delicious one, worth seeking out. If you are having trouble finding it, then sea bream is an excellent alternative, but this simple method for roasting will work nicely with any large, firm, white fish. When fish is fresh, in my opinion, doing less is more. A beautiful side would be either of my fagiolini dishes (page 53).

1 tsp (5 mL) extra-virgin olive oil, for greasing the pan
1 4–6 lb (2–3 kg) whole dentex, cleaned
Salt and freshly ground pepper, QB

For the Sauce:
5 tbsp (75 mL) extra-virgin olive oil
12 anchovy fillets, finely chopped
2 cloves garlic, finely chopped
Zest and juice of 2 lemons
1/2 cup (125 mL) white wine
2 tbsp (30 mL) capers, packed in salt, rinsed
1 bunch fresh flat-leaf parsley, chopped

Preheat the oven to 375°F (190°C).

To start, make the sauce for the fish. Put all the sauce ingredients in a bowl and whisk briskly to combine.

With the 1 tsp (5 mL) of olive oil, grease a baking pan large enough for the fish, and lay it in lengthwise. Open the dentex and pour half of the sauce over the inside. Close it up and pour the rest on top. Season with salt and pepper. Bake for about 40 minutes, basting every 10 minutes with the pan juices.

Per 6–8 persone

COZZE CON ACETO DI VINO ROSSO
MUSSELS COOKED IN RED WINE VINEGAR

I love mussels. They have a sweet and delicate meat, and so it's not hard to persuade me to make up a pot of them. As well, they cook really fast and deliver terrific flavor. I eat this as an appetizer or a light *secondo*.

This is a basic recipe with a little spin—the addition of red wine vinegar, which is optional. You can also use this same recipe to cook clams.

3 lb (1.5 kg) mussels	1 bunch fresh flat-leaf parsley, chopped
4 tbsp (60 mL) extra-virgin olive oil	1 cup (250 mL) wine
2 cloves garlic, finely chopped	Salt, QB
Chili pepper flakes, QB	6 tbsp (90 mL) red wine vinegar

Cleaning mussels is easy. Most of the time when you get them from the fishmonger, they're already cleaned and just need a rinse. If you do find wild mussels, you'll have to scrub them to get the sand and grit off. Check your mussels for beards, those silky threads, and just tear them off. Look your mussels over. They should all be closed. If any are open, absolutely do not use them. Pick them out and toss them.

Now you're ready to go.

You'll want to make these in a deep pan with a lid.

Heat up your pan on high heat. Pour in olive oil, add garlic and chili flakes and let the mussels cook. When the garlic is slightly browned, add half of the parsley and the mussels. Put the lid on the pan to get the mussels started and give the pan a shake. After 1 minute or so, throw in the wine and some salt and put the lid back on. Let the mussels cook for a few more minutes, shaking every so often to entice them to open. After about 4 minutes, take off the lid and check to see what's going on. If most of the mussels have opened up, hit them with the red wine vinegar. Continue cooking without the lid until virtually all the mussels are open. Discard any that don't open. Sprinkle the rest of the parsley over and serve.

These mussels also taste fantastic served at room temperature.

Per 4 persone

CALAMARI RIPIENI
STUFFED SQUID

This is absolutely delicious. It is a must at our big family Christmas and Easter dinners, not because the dish is classically associated with these holidays, but because our family loves it, and there would be a riot if it weren't served.

This may look like a more complicated recipe, but in fact, once you have the ingredients ready to go, it is really easy to put together. And like most stuffings, the one for this dish is really *quanto basta*, so adjust to your taste.

The calamari is perfect for stuffing, because it's relatively neutral tasting. Props to my mom for the addition of salami, which puts this already flavorful stuffing over the top. There is a bonus to making this: It's another one of those "two-in-one" dishes. When it's finished cooking, you serve the sauce over pasta for your *primo*, and then the squid is your *secondo*.

6 medium squid, cleaned

1 cup (250 mL) bread crumbs

2 oz (60 g) spicy salami, cubed

2 oz (60 g) smoky scamorza
  cheese, cubed

1 large egg

1 large bunch fresh flat-leaf
  parsley, chopped

1 cup (250 mL) freshly grated
  Parmigiano-Reggiano cheese

4 tbsp (60 mL) extra-virgin olive oil

3 cups (750 mL) white wine

Salt and freshly ground pepper, QB

2 cloves garlic

Chili pepper flakes, QB

1 lb (500 g) linguine, cooked (optional)

You can buy the squid cleaned, but make sure it has tentacles on it.

To start, give the squid a good rinse inside and out. Cut the tentacles off and chop them finely.

To make the stuffing: In a large mixing bowl, put the chopped tentacles, bread crumbs, salami, scamorza, egg, half of the parsley, the Parmigiano, 1 tbsp (15 mL) of the olive oil, 1 cup (250 mL) of the white wine and season with some salt and pepper. Get your hands in there and thoroughly mix all the ingredients. The egg will help bind everything. Now this is what I mean about *quanto basta*: If the mixture is still a bit runny and won't hold together, you can add whatever you'd like to bind it—more cheese, more bread crumbs, etc. Or if it's too thick, add more wine—you get the idea.

Gently stuff each squid with the mixture, leaving about 1 inch (2.5 cm) space at the top. Don't overstuff because when they cook, the squid shrink; you don't want the stuffing to pop out. Seal the opening by threading a toothpick through it.

In a large frying pan, heat up the remaining olive oil over medium heat. Add the garlic, chili flakes and the remaining parsley. Cook for a minute, until the garlic begins to turn slightly brown. Then add the squid and cook on all sides, until the meat becomes opaque. If some of the stuffing comes out, don't panic. It won't go to waste—it will become part of the sauce. Add the remaining wine, and salt lightly. Reduce the heat to medium-low, cover the pan with a lid, and cook for about 10 minutes, letting the wine reduce and thicken up and the stuffed squid finish cooking. Then remove the squid.

If you want to serve this with linguine, reserve the sauce and toss with the hot, cooked pasta just before serving.

Per 6 persone

CALAMARI FRITTI
FRIED SQUID

Calamari Fritti has been a staple of every bar and many, many restaurants, whether they're Italian themed or not, seemingly forever. It's a great snack or light dinner when you make it at home for yourself. A couple of musts: I know I say this all the time, but for this recipe, using extra-virgin olive oil is essential. Remember, the oil will add flavor to the dish, so you want this element. And you don't need a deep fryer to make Calamari Fritti well, so don't use that as an excuse! You just need a deep frying pan. The oil has to be hot, so that the squid fries quickly. You want a crisp outside and a tender inside. Another tip: make sure that you don't overcoat the rings.

When I was growing up, this dish was a mainstay of our Christmas and Easter table, when my mom would make them in bulk in advance. But for best results, especially for that crispy coating, I recommend eating these as soon as they're made.

8 squid, cleaned	1 cup (250 mL) bread crumbs
2 cups (500 mL) milk	Salt and freshly ground pepper, QB
1 cup (250 mL) flour	3 cups (750 mL) extra-virgin olive oil

Cut the squid into rings of about 1/2 inch (1 cm) and let them rest in a bowl of milk, along with the tentacles, for 5 minutes.

Mix the flour, bread crumbs, salt and pepper in a bowl.

Take the squid out of the milk bath and shake gently to remove any excess liquid. Gently dip the squid into the flour mixture, coating evenly. Remove them to a plate, shaking off any excess flour.

Heat up the olive oil in a deep pan until the oil just starts to smoke. (Note: This is my "scientific" method; I don't use a thermometer.) Gently put some of the calamari into the hot oil. Don't overcrowd the pan. Fry until golden and crisp. With a slotted spoon, remove the calamari and place them on a plate lined with paper towel. Immediately hit them with salt. Enjoy!

Per 4–6 persone

SPIEDINI DI PESCE
FISH KEBOBS

This is all about the beauty of fresh grilled fish and not covering it up with heavy marinades or sauces. When it comes to fresh fish, less is more.

12 skewers (if using wooden skewers, first soak them in water for about 20 minutes)
1 lb (500 g) skinless swordfish
1 lb (500 g) skinless salmon
24 shrimp, peeled and deveined (see page 259)

24 cherry tomatoes
4 tbsp (60 mL) extra-virgin olive oil
Salt and freshly ground pepper, QB
2 lemons, quartered

Heat grill to high. Cut swordfish and salmon into 24 1-inch (2.5 cm) cubes in total. Thread onto the skewers, alternating with the shrimp and tomatoes.

Brush your kebobs with olive oil and season with salt and pepper. Grill until the fish is opaque, around 3 minutes on each side. When they come off the grill, squeeze lemon juice over the kebobs. Serve immediately.

Per 4–6 persone

Dolci

Everyone needs a little *dolcezza*! I'm not big on making desserts, mostly because I like to freestyle when I cook, and baking doesn't allow you to take that approach. But these desserts are simple enough for people with my temperament, absolutely delicious, and somewhat forgiving.

TORTA DI MELE DELLE ROCCETTES
THE ROCCETTES' APPLE YOGURT CAKE

This is a perfect cake, in my opinion. It's not too sweet, so you can serve it as a dessert or—as I like it—on a lazy Sunday morning with a cappuccino. The yogurt makes it super moist. My daughters, Emma and Giorgia (aka the Roccettes), are absolutely in love with it. And now part of our Sunday ritual is sitting together with our cake, me with a cappuccino and the paper, and the twins with their steamed milk and coloring books—just hanging out. And so, even if this recipe weren't so delicious, the ritual alone would make it a perfect cake.

1 1/3 cups (325 mL) flour	2 eggs
1/4 tsp (1 mL) cinnamon	1/2 cup (125 mL) yogurt
1/4 tsp (1 mL) salt	2 apples, peeled, cored and thinly sliced
1/2 cup (125 mL) sugar	Zest of 1 lemon
7 oz (200 g) butter, melted	1/3 cup (75 mL) sugar, for the topping

Preheat the oven to 350°F (180°C). Butter an 8-inch (20 cm) baking pan.

Mix together the flour, cinnamon and salt.

In a separate bowl beat the 1/2 cup (125 mL) sugar and melted butter with a hand mixer until light and airy. Add the eggs one at a time, beating for a few minutes after each addition. Reduce the speed of your hand mixer and add a third of the flour mixture, mix that in, and then mix in half of the yogurt. Repeat until the ingredients have been mixed together. At this point, stir in the sliced apples and the lemon zest. Pour the batter into the buttered baking pan. Smooth it out with a spatula. Sprinkle the 1/3 cup (75 mL) sugar on top. Bake for about 40 minutes, until the top is golden and a fork you poke into it comes out clean.

Per papà e Giorgia e Emma

PROFITEROLES AL LIMONE
LEMON PUFFS

This may be the fussiest recipe in the book, because it does require a few steps and some technique, but it's nothing that you can't master. And the results are worth it. The dessert is light, lemony and elegant.

For the Lemon Cream:
3 3/4 cups (925 mL) milk
1 tsp (5 mL) vanilla extract
6 large (or 8 small) egg yolks
3/4 cup (175 mL) sugar
1 cup (250 mL) flour
Zest of 2 lemons

For the Puffs:
1 cup (250 mL) butter
2 cups (500 mL) water
2 cups (500 mL) flour
1/2 tsp (2 mL) salt
8 eggs
1 cup (250 mL) whipping cream (35%)
1/4 cup (60 mL) sugar

For the Lemon Cream: Pour the milk and vanilla extract into a medium saucepan over medium-high heat. Scald the milk by bringing it to just under a boil. While the milk is heating, whisk together the egg yolks and the 3/4 cup (175 mL) sugar in a large bowl until the mixture becomes creamy and pale. Add the flour, mixing slowly until it's all combined. Next, take your hot milk and pour that in, stirring continuously until it's well incorporated. Pour the whole thing back into the saucepan and put it back on the stove over medium heat. Continue stirring for about 5 minutes or until the mixture reaches the consistency of a thick pastry cream. Remove from the heat, stir in one-third of the lemon zest and set aside. Cover with a piece of parchment paper, so that it doesn't form a skin while it cools.

For the Puffs: Preheat the oven to 375°F (190°C). Put the butter and water into a heavy-bottomed saucepan over medium-high heat and bring to a boil. Remove from the heat and add the flour and salt, stirring constantly for 5 to 10 minutes, until the mixture is smooth and shiny. Once it pulls away from the sides of the pan and forms a ball, add the eggs, one at a time, stirring constantly until each is incorporated. Now use either a pastry sleeve or a teaspoon to drop the batter onto a greased baking sheet, about a generous teaspoon (7 mL) for each puff. Keep them about 2 inches (5 cm) apart, because the dough will double in size as it bakes. Bake for about 30 minutes or until puffed and lightly browned. Remove from the oven, transfer to a rack and let cool.

Into a clean bowl, pour your whipping cream and the 1/4 cup (60 mL) of sugar and lightly whip up the mixture. Fold in another one-third of the lemon zest. Now fold half of the whipped cream into the lemon cream. Cut the tops off the cooled puffs, fill with the lemon cream and gently replace the tops.

To serve: Put as many as you'd like per serving on a plate, and top each with a bit of the lightly whipped cream and the remaining lemon zest.

Makes about 30 puffs

TORTA CAPRESE

This is a very typical Neapolitan dessert that was invented by my family. No, just kidding. But it's so good that I wish we had. It actually originated on the Isle of Capri, hence the name Torta Caprese. It is a flourless cake and, like the Torta di Mele delle Roccettes (page 341), is great for either dessert or breakfast. If you're looking for a chocolate fix, look no further.

1 1/3 cups (325 mL) blanched almonds, roughly chopped	1 cup (250 mL) sugar
	1 tbsp (15 mL) vanilla extract
6 oz (175 g) good-quality bittersweet chocolate, chopped	Zest of 1 lemon
	6 eggs, separated
1 cup (250 mL) butter	Icing sugar, for sprinkling

Preheat an oven to 350°F (180°C). Line a 9-inch (23 cm) springform pan with parchment paper. Lightly butter the paper.

I like to put the almonds on a chopping board and chop them with a mezzaluna. I want various textures, so that you find little chunks of almond in the finished torta. Whatever you do, don't chop them too fine—you want the coarse texture.

In a double boiler, slowly melt the chocolate and butter, then let cool slightly.

Whisk in the sugar and vanilla extract. Then fold in the ground almonds and lemon zest, and mix until combined. Keep mixing, adding the egg yolks one at a time.

In a separate bowl, beat the egg whites until they form stiff peaks, and then gently fold them into the almond-chocolate mixture.

Pour the batter into the prepared springform pan. Bake on the middle rack of the oven for 50 minutes or until the cake begins to pull away from the side of the pan. You can also test it by inserting a toothpick or a knife point into the center. If it comes out clean or with moist crumbs, then you know it's done.

Let it cool and sprinkle the top with icing sugar. Serve with some fresh whipped cream.

Per 10 persone

I BISCOTTI DI NONNA JOSIE
GRANDMA JOSIE'S TWICE-BAKED COOKIES

One of the benefits of having kids is that their grandmothers show up with all the treats you used to enjoy when you were little. So now my mom is showing up with her fantastic biscotti for my kids. These twice-baked cookies are perfect for dipping in milk, coffee or even a Vin Santo.

3 cups (750 mL) flour

A pinch of salt

2 tsp (10 mL) baking powder

1/2 cup (125 mL) extra-virgin olive oil

1/2 cup (125 mL) sugar

2 tsp (10 mL) vanilla extract

4 large eggs

Zest of 1 lemon

2 cups (500 mL) roasted almonds

Heat your oven to 350°F (180°C).

Line a cookie sheet with parchment paper and set aside.

In a bowl, combine the flour, salt and baking powder and set that aside.

In a large bowl, mix the oil, sugar and vanilla extract until they're well blended. Then beat in the eggs. Gradually stir the flour mixture into the egg mixture. Add the lemon zest and roasted almonds. Mix until everything has come together to make a nice cookie dough.

Divide the dough in half and form two loaves. Gently flatten them with the palm of your hand. They'll be about 3 x 12 inches (7.5 x 30 cm) each. Put them on the parchment-lined cookie sheet and bake for 30 minutes, or until the loaves are light brown. Take them out of the oven and let cool for 10 minutes. Reduce the temperature to 300°F (150°C). Remove each loaf to a cutting board and, with a serrated knife, cut each of the loaves into individual slices about 3/4 inch (2 cm) thick. Lay the slices on the parchment paper, put them back into the oven and bake for another 10 minutes, or until golden and dry. Remove from the oven and let cool.

These will keep in a tightly closed cookie tin for about a week. My mom freezes them in baggies and brings them out as she needs them.

Makes 24 cookies

PESCHE UBRIACHE
DRUNKEN PEACHES

This is a very elegant dessert to make when peaches are in season and abundant. The combination of spices adds an intriguing complexity to complement the sweet peaches.

4 peaches
1 star anise
1 tsp (5 mL) cinnamon
2 cardamom pods
4 cups (1 L) red wine
Freshly whipped cream, QB
Zest of 1 lemon

Blanch your peaches by cutting a small "x" in the bottom of each one and then dropping them into boiling water. After about 1 minute, remove them, and when they're cool enough to handle, peel off the skin with a paring knife or even just your hands.

Cut the peaches into eighths, discarding the pits.

Put the star anise, cinnamon and cardamom pods into a coffee grinder or blender and process until you have a fine powder.

Pour your favorite red wine—a Chianti works well—into a pot, add the spices and bring the liquid to a boil. Lower to a simmer and cook until it's reduced by two-thirds, or thickened and syrupy. Take it off the heat. Add the peaches and let the mixture rest for 1/2 hour.

To serve, pour some of the wine reduction onto a plate. Add slices of peaches, top with freshly whipped cream and sprinkle with lemon zest.

Per 4 persone

TORTA ALL'OLIO D'OLIVA
OLIVE OIL CAKE

You'll find this cake served at all times of the day in Tuscany, especially during the olive oil season. A lot of family-run trattorias serve it with coffee in the morning and then offer it as dessert at lunch and dinner. It's moist and simple, and I absolutely love it.

1 large orange
5 eggs yolks
3/4 cup (175 mL) sugar, plus an additional 2 tbsp (30 mL) for sprinkling
3/4 cup (175 mL) extra-virgin olive oil, plus additional for greasing the pan

1 cup (250 mL) flour, sifted
4 egg whites
A pinch of salt
1/2 cup (125 mL) pine nuts

Preheat the oven to 350°F (180°C) and line a 9-inch (23 cm) springform pan with parchment paper.

Zest the orange and finely chop the zest. Squeeze half the orange, reserving the juice.

Put the egg yolks and sugar in a large bowl and beat with your hand mixer on high speed for about 2 minutes, until creamy and pale.

Lower the speed and add the olive oil and orange juice, beating until everything is combined. With a spatula or wooden spoon, slowly fold in the flour until fully incorporated.

In a separate bowl, beat the egg whites with a pinch of salt until they form stiff peaks. Gently fold the whites into the yolk mixture a bit at a time, until everything is combined. Don't overmix. Pour the batter into the springform pan. Pick up the pan and gently knock it on the counter a few times to burst any air bubbles. Sprinkle the top with sugar and pine nuts, and cook until the top is golden, about 45 minutes.

Per 10 persone

TIRAMISÙ AL VIN SANTO
LAZY MAN'S TIRAMISÙ

Icall this my lazy man's tiramisù, but there's nothing slothful about the creamy mascarpone merging with the crunch of cookies infused with the liqueur and topped with as much chocolate as makes you happy. I call it lazy because it doesn't take much time to put together, and it doesn't have to sit like a classic tiramisù before you can eat it.

If you can't get your hands on cantucci (or cantuccini) cookies or Vin Santo liqueur, you can substitute regular biscotti and a port wine or even Grand Marnier.

1 lb (500 g) cantucci or cantuccini cookies	1 lb (500 g) mascarpone cheese
1 cup (250 mL) Vin Santo liqueur (or QB)	2 tbsp (30 mL) sugar (or QB)
	3 1/2 oz (100 g) bittersweet chocolate, chopped (optional)

Bash up your cookies. You can just smack them with the bottom of a pan (which is very satisfying if you've had a bad day) or chop them with a knife (which can make you feel very "cheffy" if you're in the right mood). Put the broken cookies into a cake pan and then pour half of the Vin Santo, or your liqueur of choice, over them. The goal here isn't to drown the cookies. You want to give them flavor, but still have them retain their crunch.

In a separate bowl, mix together the mascarpone, sugar to taste, and the rest of the liqueur, again to taste. If you want, you can also chop up some chocolate and add it here, or you can wait until the end and sprinkle it on top of the individual servings. I've done both and one method isn't better than the other. Whatever you choose, mix this well, so that everything is nicely incorporated, and then spread the whole thing over the cookies, so that they're fully covered. You can, if you want, go one step further and sprinkle chopped chocolate and chopped cookie bits over the whole thing. You can serve this tiramisù immediately.

Per 6 persone

ZABAGLIONE CON FRUTTI DI BOSCO
ZABAGLIONE WITH MIXED FRESH BERRIES

This version is a fun spin on the old-school recipe: it substitutes espresso for the Marsala wine. My mom used to give us shots of a raw, sugarless zabaglione and Marsala every morning before we went to school. It must be the Italian version of a chewable vitamin, because all of the Italian kids got the same shot from their mothers.

4 large egg yolks
4 tbsp (60 mL) sugar
1/2 cup (125 mL) espresso, cooled
1 cup (250 mL) fresh blueberries
1 cup (250 mL) fresh raspberries

You are going to cook this over a pot of simmering water, which is called a *bain-marie*. The pot should be wide enough so that your mixing bowl can rest on it without falling in. And you don't want the water to touch the bottom of the bowl.

So, bring your water to a nice simmer.

In a steel bowl, whisk together egg yolks, sugar and espresso. Now put the bowl over the pot of simmering water and continue whisking vigorously until the zabiglione is blended, creamy and slightly foamy, which takes just a few minutes. You want to keep whisking so that the eggs don't cook and turn into scrambled eggs. If the temperature seems too hot, take the bowl off the water.

Once the zabaglione is done, serve it immediately, either on its own or poured over mixed berries.

Per 4 persone

CHEESECAKE DI CARLA
CARLA'S CHEESECAKE

My friend Carla is a great pastry chef in Positano, on the Amalfi coast. She makes all the cakes for Hotel Buca di Bacco and always insists that I have a slice or two of what she's just freshly made. This is her cheesecake, and it's the best I've ever had.

For the Crust:
1/2 cup (125 mL) toasted almonds
1 1/2 cups (375 mL) crushed graham crackers
1/4 cup (60 mL) sugar
1 cup (250 mL) unsalted butter, melted

For the Filling:
1 lb (500 g) cream cheese, softened
8 oz (250 g) mascarpone
4 eggs, separated
1 cup (250 mL) sugar
1 cup (250 mL) whipping cream (35%)
1 tsp (5 mL) vanilla extract
1/4 cup (60 mL) cocoa powder

Preheat oven to 350° F (180°C) and butter a 10-inch (25 cm) springform pan.

To make the crust, whiz together the almonds, graham crackers, sugar and butter in a food processor until the mixture is slightly moist and uniform. Reserve 1/4 cup (60 mL) for the topping. Press the rest of mixture into the bottom of the prepared pan and 1/2 inch (1 cm) up the side.

For the filling, in a large bowl, beat the cream cheese and mascarpone with a wooden spoon until smooth and creamy. Then add the egg yolks, one at a time, beating well as you add each one. Then beat in the sugar, cream and vanilla.

In a separate bowl, beat the egg whites until they just hold stiff peaks and gently fold them into the cream cheese–mascarpone mixture. Spoon the filling onto the crust, smoothing the top with a spatula.

Mix the reserved crumb mixture with the cocoa powder and sprinkle this evenly on top. Bake on the lowest rack of the oven for 70 minutes.

Turn off the oven and let the cake rest for 1 hour. Then cover and chill in the fridge for at least 3 hours. Let it stand at room temperature for 30 minutes before serving.

Per 10 persone

GRANITA DI LIMONE
LEMON GRANITA

I had one of my most memorable street food surprises where I least expected to find it. One hot, blazingly sunny June day, we were driving down the hilly, winding road out of Ravello, along the Amalfi coast. We turned the corner and there on the shoulder, at a point where three roads met, was a guy selling lemon granita from a little refrigerated cart. He charged about 50 cents for a cup of what turned out to be heaven on a spoon. It was perfect—not too tart, not too sweet—and incredibly refreshing. His version had tiny bits of frozen lemon rind that added beautiful little bursts of extra flavor. I teased him that his prices were way too low for what he offered, and he smiled. "*Non ti preoccupà*," he said. "Don't worry. It's only local lemons, water and sugar. Why should I charge more? I like doing this." (If I lived in Amalfi, I could see myself stopping here twice a day— on my way to and from work!) When I asked him for his recipe, he said, "No problem: Squeeze some lemons, add water and sugar. Taste it. If it's not too sweet, it's good. Let it freeze, and once it's done, scrape it and serve!"

CHESTNUTS

CASTAGNE UBRIACHE
DRUNKEN CHESTNUTS

I love roasted chestnuts. In Italy, you can tell when fall is thinking about turning to winter by the smell of roasting chestnuts wafting from the little carts on the street. They're a tradition at Christmas.

When friends drop in, I like to make this treat. If you think that roasted chestnuts are a thing of beauty, wait until you taste what happens when they spend a little time hanging out with some rum.

24 roasted chestnuts, peeled
2 tbsp (30 mL) sugar
1/2 cup (125 mL) rum (or QB)

Roasting chestnuts is easy. Make a slit in them so they don't explode as they cook. You can put them in an oven at 400°F (200°C) for about 20 minutes. Or if you have access to an open fire, that's even better. You can buy a special pan to cook them in that has holes in the bottom to let the flames get right in there, which adds a smokiness to the nuts. Or you can roast the chestnuts on a stovetop in a dry frying pan on medium-high heat, shaking the pan every so often. It should take about 30 minutes.

Once they've been roasted, let them cool just enough that you can handle them to peel.

Put the peeled roasted chestnuts in a large mixing bowl and add the sugar and rum.

Now you're going to flambé this, so be careful. Here's how you do it: Light a match. Tilt your bowl so that some of the rum is exposed to the flame. It will light up, and the alcohol will burn off fairly quickly.

While it's flaming, stir continuously to dissolve the sugar, until the rum has reduced to a thick syrup and the flame has died out. Serve immediately.

Per 4 persone

FRITTELLE DI CASTAGNE
CHESTNUT FRITTERS

Chestnut flour, which in Tuscany is sometimes called *farina dolce*, is a very versatile flour. In fact, traditionally polenta called for chestnut flour, which is used for everything from pastas to pancakes to desserts and cakes.

Poor Tuscan farmers would rely on this flour to help get them through the long winter. It's healthy, and it's getting a lot of press these days because it's gluten-free.

For an easy-to-make and delicious example of why it's called "sweet flour," try these fritters. To fry them, I would use only extra-virgin olive oil, because it makes them that much tastier.

1 3/4 cups (425 mL) chestnut flour
2 cups (500 mL) water
A pinch of salt

Extra-virgin olive oil, for deep frying
Icing sugar (QB)

Mix the chestnut flour and the water together until the mixture is smooth and just slightly thicker than a pancake batter. Add a pinch of salt and give it a good mix.

Heat up the olive oil in a deep frying pan over high heat. Just before the oil starts to smoke, start gently dropping small ladlefuls of your fritter batter into it. Don't overcrowd the pan. Cook until they're golden on both sides. As they're done, put them on a plate covered with paper towel to soak up any excess oil. Plate them and sprinkle with icing sugar.

Per 6 persone

CASTAGNACCIO
TUSCAN CHESTNUT PIZZA

This is a classic fall dessert in Tuscany that's made from chestnut flour. If you haven't tried it, I'd urge you to give this a shot. The flour's nutty, sweet, smoky, mellow flavor works beautifully with this combination of sweet raisins, pine nuts and earthy rosemary. Not too sweet and very satisfying.

2 cups (500 mL) chestnut flour	6 tbsp (90 mL) extra-virgin
2 tbsp (30 mL) sugar	olive oil
A pinch of salt	1/2 cup (125 mL) raisins
2 1/2 cups (625 mL) water	1/2 cup (125 mL) pine nuts
Zest of 1 orange	Leaves of 2 sprigs fresh rosemary

Preheat your oven to 400°F (200°C).

Mix together the chestnut flour, sugar, salt, water and two-thirds of the orange zest. Make sure you mix it well so there are no lumps. You're aiming for a pancake batter texture—not too runny, not too thick, and with a silky-smooth consistency. Pour your olive oil into a large round pizza pan and put it in the oven for 5 minutes to heat up the olive oil.

The oil and the pan have to be extremely hot—so hot that when the batter goes in, the whole thing sizzles.

Carefully take the pan out of the oven. Pour your batter into the center and let it flow out to the edges. Sprinkle the raisins, pine nuts, rosemary and the final one-third of the orange zest on top. Bake for about 20 minutes or until the top is golden and the castagnaccio pulls away from the sides.

Per 10–12 persone

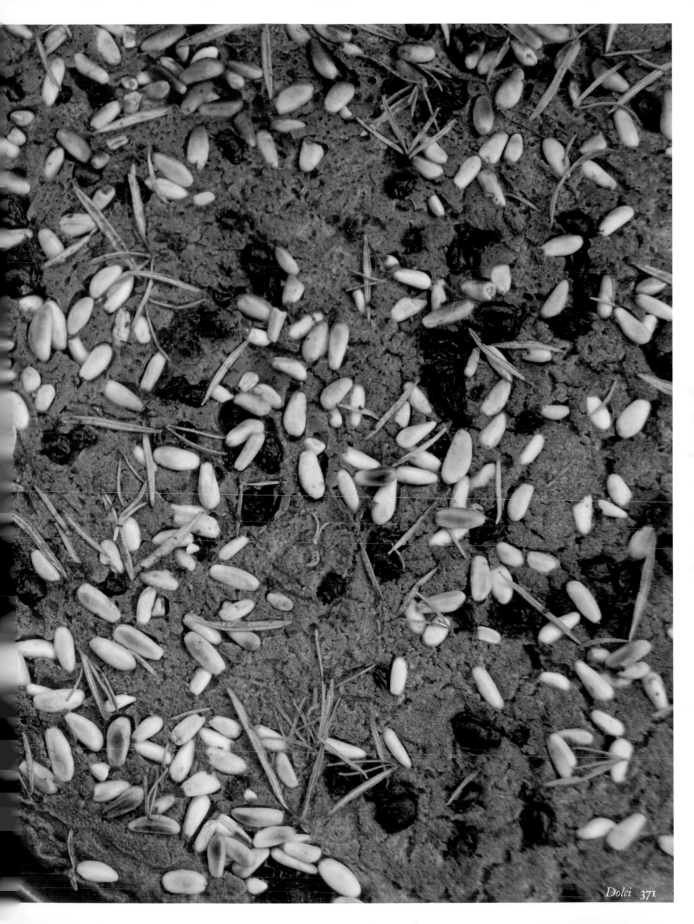

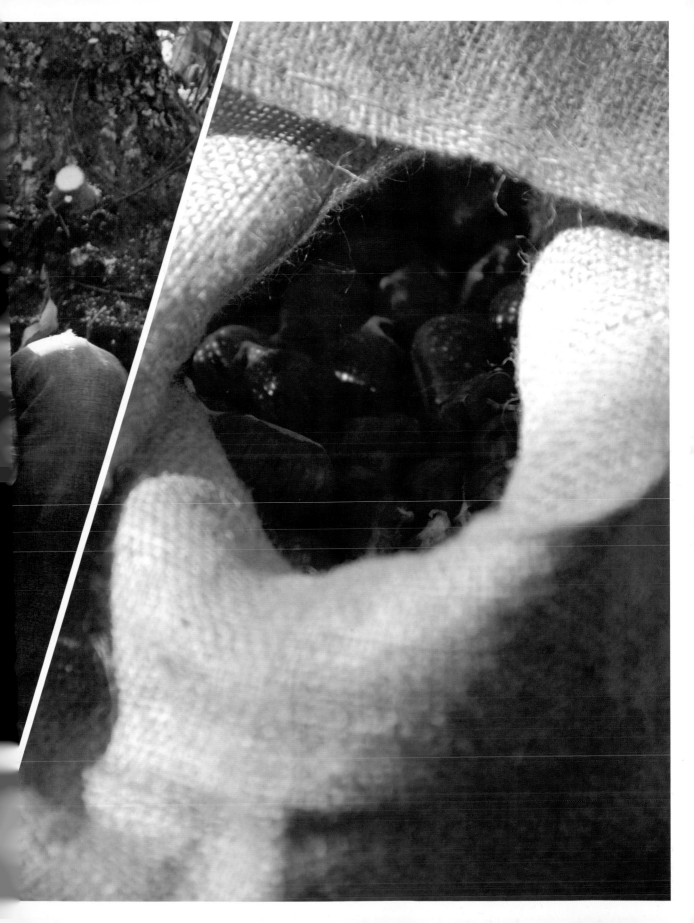

FICHI E MANDORLE AL FORNO CON GRAPPA
BAKED FIGS AND ALMONDS WITH GRAPPA

I make this treat a lot in the late fall and winter. It's quick and easy, and so it's perfect to whip together when friends drop in unexpectedly.

Dried figs, QB

Almonds, QB

Sugar, QB

A good splash of grappa

Preheat oven to 400°F (200°C). With a paring knife, cut a slit in each fig, making sure to keep the fruit intact. Press 1 or 2 almonds into each fig and then press it together to close.

Put the figs in a baking dish and sprinkle them with sugar. Add more almonds over top and a splash of grappa. Bake for 20 minutes, or until the figs are slightly golden.

ESPRESSO x 3

After a meal, and especially after dessert, an espresso is a must. Here are three more ways of properly finishing a meal.

ESPRESSO CORRETTO

1 shot espresso
1 shot grappa or sambuca

Into your shot of espresso, add grappa or sambuca, QB.

ESPRESSO CON PANNA

1 single long shot espresso
Whipped cream

Into a cappuccino cup or small glass, pour your espresso and top with a dollop of freshly whipped cream.

GELATO AFFOGATO

1 single long shot espresso
Vanilla ice cream

Put a scoop of premium vanilla ice cream into a cup or small serving bowl and pour a shot of hot espresso over top.

Mille Grazie!

To the talented Karen Gordon, for your passion and unwavering commitment to the project and your creativity in capturing my voice. Thank you for always being there to bounce ideas off of and for all your suggestions. And you still make me laugh!

Francesco Lastrucci, my good friend and brilliant photographer, your pictures are all so deliciously beautiful! Your work has heart and soul. I look forward to our next adventure. . . . We have way too much fun eating our way through Italy. *E vai!*

Clint Rogerson, a huge thank you for your art direction and for bringing great style and a gorgeous new look to this book. Great job! It was fun, and you always had brilliant tunes in the office. I'm now a country music fan!

To my Canadian publisher HarperCollins Canada: You are all so awesome! Thanks to my editor, Kirsten Hanson, for all your hard work and for honoring my vision and style; to Neil Erickson and Noelle Zitzer, for always being there to answer my questions; and to copy editor Barbara Kamienski, for your amazing thoroughness and commitment to detail. To my US publisher, Clarkson Potter, and editor Rica Allannic, thanks for all your support and belief in this project and for taking a chance on me.

Joanna McIntyre, your encouragement, advice and feedback keeps me grounded. Your attention to style and detail is incredible. (Yes, Art and God are in the details!)

My talented assistant Lauren Greenway, you contribute on so many levels, and you always knew where to find that one picture we needed! Lucas K. Labrecque—friend, editor and associate producer—you are always there to help out. Thanks for being willing to go through a wall for me!

To the entire Planeta family, especially Francesca and Alessio Planeta: you have always welcomed me with sincere Sicilian hospitality, food and fantastic wine! *Bacioni!*

The entire staff at Hotel Villa Maria and Hotel Giordano in Ravello, and especially Carla Rispolli, Giuseppe, Francesco and Vincenzo Palumbo (a.k.a. "Professore"). Since the first day we met, you have treated Nina and me like family. Thank you for all your support, encouragement and inspiration. *Un abbraccio!*

To *la famiglia* Galli: Bernardo, for your humor, hard work and organization on our Italian productions and for becoming an official *"scrocco"*; the beautiful Gioia, for your love of food, for sharing recipes and for extending your kitchen and table to me; and Dr. Paolo Galli, for always being there for the Roccettes and quick to open a bottle of your mysterious prosecco for me!

Grazie to my mom and dad, who always kept Italian traditions alive in our home and from a young age taught me the importance of food and eating together. Love you. To my beautiful family—my wife, Nina, and my daughters, Emma and Giorgia—thank you for your constant support. You make my life very *dolce!* You are my inspiration. I love you very much!

David

INDEX